The NOBLE PHILOSOPHER

CONDORCET AND THE ENLIGHTENMENT

With an excerpt from the
*Sketch for a Historical Picture of the
Progress of the Human Mind*

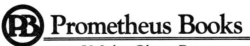

Prometheus Books

59 John Glenn Drive
Buffalo, New York 14228-2197

Published 1994 by Prometheus Books

98 97 96 95 94   5 4 3 2 1

Library of Congress Cataloging-in-Publication Data

Goodell, Edward
    The noble philosopher : Condorcet and the Enlightenment / Edward Goodell.
        p.   cm.
    Includes bibliographical references.
    ISBN 0-87975-875-9 (cloth : alk. paper)
    1. Condorcet, Jean-Antoine-Nicolas de Caritat, marquis de, 1743–1794. 2. Enlightenment—France. 3. France—Intellectual life—18th century. I. Title.
B1997.G67   1994
194—dc20   93-49525
                                                                             CIP

Printed in the United States of America on acid-free paper.

Contents

5

Part Three: Condorcet the Man—Friends, Marriage, and His Works Before the Revolution (1765–1789)

Part Four: Condorcet and the French Revolution

Part Five: *Sketch for a Historical Picture of the Progress of the Human Mind*

Appendix: "The Tenth Stage: The Future Progress of the Human Mind" —the Final Chapter of the *Sketch*

Preface

He was the last of the illustrious line of French philosophers called *philosophes,* who graced eighteenth-century France and enriched the world with the message of "enlightenment." As that century was about to become another chapter in history, Marie-Jean-Antoine-Nicolas Caritat, Marquis de Condorcet, bequeathed to posterity his *Sketch for a Historical Picture of the Progress of the Human Mind,*[1] a work addressed to the proposition that the human race is progressing toward an ultimate state of perfection.[2]

In a very real sense the *Sketch* was a testament to that conviction. It was written during the tumult of the French Revolution while Condorcet, fearing death at the hands of the Jacobins, was hiding in the pension kept by a Madame Vernet.[3] Despite the fact that as he wrote the *Sketch* he was a victim of humanity's capacity for fanaticism and cruelty, his faith in human nature and its capacity to reason rationally remained unshaken. There is no suggestion in the book of the often mindless violence of the Revolution nor of the critical nature of his own unwarranted predicament.

7

The contents of the *Sketch,* as well as the title, indicate that it was probably intended to be only the introduction to a larger work which he hoped to complete in the event that he eluded his enemies and survived long enough to develop his theme. As he said in the last chapter of the *Sketch,* "In other words, do not all these observations which I propose to develop further in my book show that the moral goodness of man, the necessary consequence of his constitution, is capable of indefinite[4] perfection like all his other faculties."[5]

During a period of about nine months from July 1793 to March 1794, Condorcet sketched his legacy on progress and perfectibility, undoubtedly driven by the fear that he might not have the time to do more.[6] That fear, if it was in fact entertained by Condorcet, would nevertheless have been warranted, as the events that followed the completion of the *Sketch* established.

Suspecting that his hiding place was being watched and worried that Madame Vernet might suffer for sheltering him, Condorcet deposited his manuscript with her and, brushing aside her protests, left in disguise. A few days later, while asking for food at an inn on the outskirts of Paris, he was recognized, arrested, and imprisoned at Bourg-La-Reine. On the following day, March 29, 1794, he was found dead in his cell.[7] The cause of his death has not been determined. He was then only fifty-one, but a full and distinguished career had preceded that sudden and premature end.

Those fifty-one years were lived during a period of tremendous intellectual ferment and development, nothing less than that remarkable chapter in the history of the human mind known as the Enlightenment. It was also a period of transition and, ultimately, of radical and turbulent change, in the political and social structures of France, as the absolute monarchy collapsed and the first republic was born.

Louis XIV, the autocratic Sun King—the Grand Monarch—had welded France into an absolute monarchy during his long reign, extending seventy-two years from his accession in 1643 to his death in 1715. His two successors were his great grandson, Louis XV, and the latter's grandson, Louis XVI, whose combined reigns covered a period of seventy-eight years from 1715 to the execution of Louis XVI in 1793. Lacking the mentality, the strength of character, and the iron will of their predecessor, they managed to preside over the dissolution of the monarchy that had been bequeathed to them.

Condorcet's life spanned thirty-one years of the reign of Louis XV (1743 to 1774) and all of the reign of Louis XVI. In that critical period of change from monarchy to republic, he was an active participant in both the intellectual renaissance of the Enlightenment and in the establishment of the republic.

A descendant of the ancient family of Caritat, Condorcet was born in Picardy, the northwest section of France that borders on the English Channel. Its principal seaport is Calais, on the strait of Dover, a center of communication with England since the Middle Ages, and home of Rodin's great bronze monument commemorating its inhabitants and named "The Burghers of Calais."

The Caritat family belonged to the hereditary order of the nobility known as the *noblesse d'épée* or nobility of the sword, superior in social status to that other order of the nobility known as the *noblesse de robe*.[8] Essentially the vocation of the *noblesse d'épée* was military, soldiering in the service of the monarchy. Commerce and trade were considered by this order of the nobility to be unsuitable as occupations. Condorcet's father, true to his heritage, was a soldier—a soldier who died in battle while his son, the philosopher to be, was an infant.[9]

It is interesting to speculate that had his father lived and directed his upbringing, Condorcet might have followed the hallowed traditions of the *noblesse d'épée* and become, like his father, an army officer; alternatively, he might have led the fruitless life of a courtier in Paris or Versailles and now be long since forgotten. But the drive of a powerful mind, the determination of a strong character, and perhaps a touch of his maternal bourgeois background propelled him from the sword to the pen, and a life far removed from a military career of obedience to one as an intellectual and a reformer.

In accordance with the custom of the day Condorcet received his education from the Jesuits at their college in Rheims and subsequently at the Jesuit College de Navarre in Paris. Despite the religious auspices of his education, the most interesting offering in the college curriculum for Condorcet was mathematics, for which he demonstrated such an affinity that he considered it as a career. At the age of twenty-two he submitted to the Academy of Sciences, an "Essay on Integral Calculus," which earned high praise from the renowned d'Alembert, one of the great men of the Enlightenment who became his mentor and friend. He gravitated quickly into the company of many outstanding intellectuals of the period, who recognized him as a thinker and personality worthy of their attention and company.

In 1769, at the age of twenty-six, he became a member of the Academy of Sciences. When he was thirty-four he was elected permanent secretary of the Academy of Sciences, and five years later, at the age of thirty-nine, he was elected to the French Academy.

Perhaps his status as an intellectual is best evidenced by that ultimate accolade of recognition in eighteenth-century France —his acceptance as a member of its salon society. The center of salon society was Paris, then the capital of the world of culture. The salons were the fashionable, exclusive, unofficial institutions for the free expression and exchange of ideas by the distinguished personalities of the day, who here felt uninhibited by the restraints of a social order in which monarchical and clerical influences were still dominant.

The presiding geniuses of the salon world were women of distinction, elegant in manners and mind, highly intelligent, always charming, and, not infrequently, gifted with beauty as well as brilliance and wit. The great ladies of the salons attracted and brought together not only the best minds of France, but those from other countries on the Continent, as well as England and even distant America.[10] Admission to their homes and acceptance by the "chairperson" of the board was eagerly sought but not lightly granted. That award of merit had to be earned by quality of mind.

Among the high priestesses of this Parisian world of culture, scintillating conversation, and free expression of ideas was Julie de Lespinasse,[11] to whose salon Condorcet was invited and to which he became a valued addition. The basis of Condorcet's acceptance was, in part, a tribute to the quality of his mind and character. Julie de Lespinasse soon came to value not only his intellect, which she considered second only to d'Alembert's, but even more the warmth of his personality and benevolence.[12] This tribute was a recognition of Condorcet's status in the life of the Age of Enlightenment as one justly entitled to be called a *philosophe.*

Philosophe is neither a misspelling nor a precious spelling of the word philosopher. It is, of course, the French word for philosopher. But in relation to eighteenth-century France the word has a special flavor and significance. Philosophes did not play the role or fit the image of traditional philosophers. They were not metaphysicians, isolated in figurative ivory towers, immersed in profound thought high above the madding crowd and the everyday affairs of life. They were, it is true, thinkers with a definite philosophy about the status and the rights of their fellow human beings, but they were also worldly, sophisticated, and practical men, who actively participated in the affairs of their society. Nevertheless they were, at the same time, idealists, fundamentally committed humanists, and leaders of the vanguard in the eighteenth-century battle against intolerance and man's inhumanity to man and for recognition of human rights and equality. The philosophes also shared a common talent—they were writers with literary ability.

In the retrospect of history—a luxury not available to Julie de Lespinasse—Condorcet's contribution of the *Sketch* to posterity has been justly appraised by the distinguished Italian philosopher, Benedetto Croce, as "The Last Will and Testament of the Eighteenth Century." To put the last will and testament of the eighteenth century in perspective, the influences that led to its writing and explain its meaning require consideration. They are the influences that inspired the thinking of the philosophes, including Condorcet, the last of the brilliant group of men who, with the help of the great ladies of the salons, fashioned an epoch justly called the Age of Enlightenment.[13]

Notes

1. Translation of *Esquisse d'un Tableau Historique des Progrès de l'Esprit Humain,* trans. June Barraclough, introduction by Stuart Hampshire (New York: Noonday Press, 1955; reprint—Westport, Conn.: Hyperion Press, 1979). All references to the *Sketch* are to this edition.

2. "The aim of the work I have undertaken," Condorcet said, "will be to show . . . that nature has set no term to the perfection of human faculties; that the perfectibility of man, is truly indefinite; and that

the progress of this perfectibility, from now onwards has no other limit than the duration of the globe upon which nature has cast us" (ibid., p. 4). See also page 184, where Condorcet said, "The real advantages that should result from this progress, of which we can entertain a hope that is almost a certainty, can have no other term than that of the absolute perfection of the human race."

3. Widow of the painter Claude-Joseph Vernet.

4. "Indefinite" is used by Condorcet in the sense of "infinite." Ibid., pp. 200 and 201.

5. Ibid., p. 193. About 1772 Condorcet began to write such a book, entitled *Tableau historique dés progrés de l'esprit humain,* but he never finished it. The *Sketch* may have been intended as an introduction to the unfinished work when it was completed. However, one cannot help but speculate that knowing the precarious nature of his situation, he might have intended it to be his message if he did not survive to complete it.

6. According to a "Note On The Text" in the Noonday/Hyperion Press translation, a note in Condorcet's hand in the text of the manuscript in the Bibliotique de l'Institut, Paris, says that the manuscript was completed on Friday, October 4, 1793. However, there are other, later texts of the *Sketch* than the one found in the Bibliotique de l'Institut that "vary considerably from it."

7. It has been speculated that he might have died as the result of the self-administration of poison (ibid., p. ix, for example).

8. The nobility of the robe was the junior order composed mainly of those members of the bourgeoisie who had achieved the rank of judicial office.

9. J. Salwyn Schapiro in *Condorcet and the Rise of Liberalism* (New York: Octagon Books, 1963), p. 66, says that Condorcet's father died "about four years after" his birth. On the other hand it has also been said that his father was killed in battle only five weeks after Condorcet's birth. See Keith Michael Baker, *Condorcet: From Natural Philosophy to Social Mathematics* (Chicago: University of Chicago Press, 1982), p. 3, where it is said that Antoine de Condorcet, a captain

of a cavalry regiment, and Condorcet's father, "met his death at Neuf-Brisach in 1742, scarcely more than a month after the birth of his son.")

10. Benjamin Franklin, for example.

11. Among the other great ladies of the eighteenth-century Parisian salons were Claudine Alexandrine de Tencin, the Marquise du Duffant, and Maria-Thérèse Geoffrin.

12. Will and Ariel Durant, *Rousseau and Revolution*, vol. 10 of *The Story of Civilization* (New York: Simon & Schuster, 1967), p. 894.

13. Although there were several men classified as philosophes who survived Condorcet, such as the Abbé Morellet (1727–1819), they did not achieve his stature or influence. For that reason Condorcet is generally considered to be entitled to the epithet of "the last philosophe."

Part One

Historical Inheritance

Introduction

Just as the fourteenth, fifteenth, and sixteenth centuries marked a great awakening and an incomparable revival of interest and accomplishment in learning, literature, and art, summed up in the word Renaissance, so the eighteenth century marked another period of liberation of the human mind. This remarkable burst of intellectual energy produced a surge of political and social ideas, which collectively historians have called the Enlightenment.

While this is a study about the Enlightenment in France and one of its French champions, the Marquis de Condorcet, it should be realized that the Enlightenment was not a phenomenon limited to France, but a wide-reaching development of the human mind which involved much of Europe and the United States.[1] Its exponents included such diverse personalities as Beccaria in Italy and Thomas Jefferson in the United States, and its ideas permeated the minds of even such absolute monarchs as Frederick the Great of Prussia and Catherine the Great of Russia, both of whom accorded their affection and friendship to Voltaire and gave financial aid to causes that he supported.

The philosophes who fashioned the Enlightenment in France were the product of an intellectual revolt that had its roots, primarily, in the life of sixteenth- and seventeenth-century France.[2] The reasoning that illuminated the eighteenth century and conferred upon it the distinction of being called the Age of Enlightenment and the Age of Reason was preceded by two centuries of repressive and oppressive domination by state and church.[3] During that time French society was subjected to control that was both authoritarian and intolerant. The independent thinker with the ingenuity and the courage to engage in self-expression was a rare personality.

Gradually the thin trickle of independent thinking, haphazardly occurring from time to time over two centuries, accumulated strength and early in the eighteenth century burst the dam that had been holding it back. While the repressive influences of the preceding centuries were not entirely dissipated, the liberated ideas of the philosophes became the mainstream of eighteenth-century thought.

This, then, is an outline of some of the factors in the philosophes' inheritance of the past that contributed to their formulation of the philosophy of the Enlightenment in France and the writing of the *Sketch*.

Notes

1. Regarding the Enlightenment in the United States, see Adrienne Koch, ed., *The American Enlightenment* (New York: George Braziller, 1962).

2. The term *philosophe* is also applied to eighteenth-century thinkers who were not French. In this study the term is used in relation to those eighteenth-century intellectuals who were French and advocates of Enlightenment.

3. The "Age of Reason" is sometimes applied to the seventeenth century as well as the eighteenth century. In this study the Age of Reason is used synonymously with the Age of Enlightenment in relation to the eighteenth century.

1

"Protestant Heresy," the Religious Wars, and the Edict of Nantes

The kings of the House of Valois presided over the fortunes and misfortunes of France during most of the sixteenth century. There were six of this line from the beginning of the century until 1589,[1] when Henry IV, also known as Henry of Navarre, became king, the first king of France from the House of Bourbon.

The last two kings of the House of Valois were Charles IX (r. 1560–1574) and Henry III (r. 1574–1589). During their occupancy of the throne of France the country was torn by eight divisive civil wars, known as the Wars of Religion[2] and also as the Huguenot Wars,[3] and by one particularly terrible day in 1572, enshrined in the annals of history as St. Bartholomew's Day. On that day Protestants were slaughtered all over France; two thousand were killed just in Paris. That day also marked the beginning of the fourth of the Wars of Religion.

The reformation had already touched France when John Calvin arrived upon the scene. Like Condorcet he, too, was born in Picardy in the year 1509. In 1536, at the age of twenty-seven, he completed his *Institutes of the Christian Religion,* one of the trailblazers of religious literature. Its tenets included the doctrine of predestination and the rejection of papal authority.

Regardless of the theological differences between Calvinism and the established church, the fact is that in a climate receptive for reform, "the success of the Protestants during the 1540s and the 1550s was remarkable."[4] They saw themselves in the position of saviors of "the lost purity of religion, blaming the church for hiding the message of Christ."[5]

Initially the leaders of French Protestantism were members of the regular clergy whose early followers were townspeople, mostly artisans and shopkeepers. However, the movement gradually attracted members of the bourgeoisie, such as lawyers and doctors, and eventually the nobility, first its women and then, under their influence, their sons and husbands.[6]

Predictably, the kings of France in the sixteenth and seventeenth centuries had an allergic reaction to deviations from conformity, accompanied by an intense compulsion to impose obedience to the established order. Beginning with the Valois kings, Francis I and Henry II, the Protestants were treated as heretics who should be exterminated by force. But as experience has demonstrated time and time again, the human mind has a high resistance level to efforts to suppress ideas or impose their acceptance. Instead of eliminating heresy, Henry II and Francis II bequeathed to their successors—Charles II and Henry III—the ingredients of animosity and hatred that erupted into the Wars of Religion beginning in 1562.

In the remaining decades of the sixteenth century, "a series of horrible and inhuman killings and massacres" occurred, "whose cumulative effect was to make co-existence between the differing religions almost impossible and which left the minority group in any particular place living in constant fear for their lives."[7] In the name of religion divisive and cruel civil wars were fought, pitting Catholics against Protestants, and at their conclusion, France was still a nation divided over the issue of religious belief. The edicts and treaties of peace[8] that followed these conflicts were, in reality, only cease fires during which the warring parties rested and recouped their strength to carry on the violent struggle between orthodoxy and "heresy."

The process of peace and some progress in the healing of wounds was facilitated by the fact that Henry IV (1589-1610) was brought up as a Protestant. As a practical man in the business of being a king he converted to Catholicism in 1593, thereby "cutting the ground from under his enemies' feet."[9] As a result of his dual experience in the roles of Protestant and Catholic he was in a position to promulgate the Edict of Nantes in 1598 and to make it effective.

It was favorable to the Protestants because, in essence, it secured for them both religious freedom and political security. In religious matters it conferred upon them freedom of private worship and also public worship in a limited number of towns. In the political sphere the edict granted Protestants full civil rights, including the right to hold public office and to have special courts composed of Catholic and Protestant judges to hear cases involving Protestants.[10] It also allowed them continued control of some two hundred towns with their own troops and fortresses, among which was the stronghold of La Rochelle.

Of course the edict pleased neither the Catholics nor the Protestants. It was accepted as a necessity. A particular source of irritation, even to the edict's creator, was the proviso granting the Protestants control of various strongholds such as La Rochelle, which, in effect, diminished the king's authority and created a state within a state.

The seventeenth century, consequently, witnessed the gradual emasculation of the edict and, finally, its revocation, through the efforts of Cardinal Richelieu and Louis XIV, both of whom were intent upon consolidating the authority of the monarchy and, in the case of the Sun King, of exorcising heresy.

Notes

1. The four members of the House of Valois who preceded Charles IX and Henry III were Louis XII (1498–1515), Francis I (1515–1547), Henry II (1547–1559), and Francis II (1559–1560).
2. The first of these wars began in 1562 and ended in 1563 and was followed by seven more in the following years: 1567–1568, 1568–1570, 1572–1573, 1574–1576, 1577, 1580, 1585–1589.
3. The word "Huguenot" is derived from the German *Eidgenossen*, meaning sworn companions or confederates.
4. Robin Briggs, *Early Modern France 1560–1715* (Oxford: Oxford University Press, 1977), p. 13.
5. Ibid., p. 13.
6. Ibid., p. 12
7. Ibid., p. 18.
8. The Edict of Amboise (March 1563); the Treaty of Saint Germain (1570); the Peace of Monsieur (1576), ratified by the Edited of Beaulieu; the Peace of Bergerac (1577).
9. Robin Briggs, *Early Modern France 1560–1715*, p. 31.
10. *Chambres de l'Etat.* Ibid., p. 33.

2

The Absolute Monarchy and the Revocation of the Edict of Nantes

Henry IV is "probably the most popular king among the French," a verdict of history based upon his "Gallic wit," his "concern for the common people," and his "gallantry."[1] Less appreciated, perhaps, in his own lifetime, he was assassinated in 1610 by a fanatic, François Ravaillac, who interpreted his policy as being anti-Catholic.[2]

He was succeeded by his son, Louis XIII (1601-1643), who was nine at the time of his father's death. The notable feature of Louis' reign was the appointment, in 1624, of Cardinal Richelieu to the office of Chief Minister, in which capacity he served until his death in 1642.

From the point of view of the monarchy Richelieu's most significant achievement was the consolidation and centralization of royal authority by the destruction of the political power of the Huguenots and the great nobles. The former was accomplished by the capture of La Rochelle in 1628 and the treaty of peace of Alais in 1629, under the terms of which the special political privileges of the Huguenots were terminated. However, "with an act of statesmanship it would be difficult to overpraise, for both its political shrewdness and its genuine humanity, Richelieu advised the king to confirm the Edict of Nantes"[3] in relation to its religious provisions. Thus, while "the Huguenots lost their fortresses and troops," they were "guaranteed liberty of conscience."[4]

Fifty-six years later that act of wise statesmanship was revoked by Louis XIV. With the stroke of a pen in 1687 he terminated the religious and political rights of the Protestants and thereby rekindled religious strife in France.

Louis XIV, as previously noted, was the Grand Monarch who welded France into an absolute monarchy during his long reign of seventy-two years (r. 1643–1715). Willful, domineering, and all-powerful within his kingdom, he was called the Sun King. Although his father died when he was just five years old, he did not begin to rule as a sovereign in fact until the death, in 1661, of Cardinal Mazarin, the successor of Cardinal Richelieu. The Grand Monarch was then twenty-three. In his first regal announcement he gave notice that he had carefully considered his philosophy of government and his position in life. A few hours after his investment with the full panoply of his authority as king, he declared that "it was his 'will never to take a prime minister' and 'to combine all the powers of a ruler in his own person.' "[5] In his memoirs, he said that as early as 1661 he "meant to have sole command in every sphere" and that he took "full responsibility before the world and all posterity, for everything that should happen in his reign."[6] That is a tall order and a heavy burden to bear but Louis XIV seemed to have no doubts about the divinity of his authority or his ability to perform. It seemed quite natural to him that the "greater part of the court, the clergy and the kingdom should proclaim him God's lieutenant upon earth."[7]

There does not appear to be historical authenticity for the attribution to Louis XIV of the expression "L'état c'est moi," but it does describe with accuracy his concept of the absoluteness of his authority as king.[8] He identified himself with France and, as Bossuet wrote later, "he believed that 'he was the whole state and the will of the people was locked in his.' "[9] The plain fact is that "there was no institution in the state with the right to prevent him from doing whatever he chose to do."[10]

In the thinking of the philosophes about the rights of man and the relationship of the state to people, the Grand Monarch's concept of the divinity of his role and of the scope of his authority represented a relic of the past, which they rejected. The new philosophy was proclaimed by the philosophes almost coincidentally with his death in 1715.

In any event Louis XIV exercised his divine right and his absolute authority in his disposition of the case of the Protestants. He reached the point of no return gradually. In the early years of his reign he expressed understanding of the reasons for what he referred to as the "so-called reform religion." In one early speech he attributed the advent of Protestantism to "the ignorance of churchmen in the last century, their luxury and debauchery," and concluded that "the new reformers were clearly telling the truth in many things of this kind . . . [although] on the other hand [they] were guilty of falsehood in all those concerned not with facts but with belief."[11]

Motivated, however, by his hunger for personal glory, his desire to eliminate division in the political and religious life of France and finally his abhorrence of what he came to conceive as intolerable heresy, he ultimately decided that "the religious unification of the kingdom would provide the crowning glory of his reign."[12] To that end he embarked on a program designed to convert Protestants to Catholicism.

The program had several facets. One inducement was waiving the payment of a tax, known as the *taille*, for those who accepted conversion to Catholicism. Those who were not susceptible to this enticement were subjected to the billeting of soldiers in their homes, a highly unpleasant device known as "dragonnades,"[13] calculated to bring the most recalcitrant to their knees. Another tactic was to interpret the Edict of Nantes as applying only to the kingdom as it was in 1598. The following consequences resulted from that interpretation: (1) Protestant houses of worship built after that date could be legally destroyed; (2) "interments not accounted for in the Edict were to take place only at night, in unconsecrated ground and with no public ceremony"; (3) special occasions of happiness such as the celebration of marriages were limited in attendance to no more than twelve people.[14]

Finally in 1685, twenty-four years after he assumed control of the government of France, he issued the Edict of Fontainebleau, which revoked the Edict of Nantes. The fictitious justification for this act was that due to the conversion process initiated by the king there were no more Protestants in France and thus there was no longer any need for the Edict of Nantes.[15]

The effect of the revocation of the Edict of Nantes was devastating. With the stroke of a pen, one million Protestants were declared to be outlaws in the country of their birth. Oppression and persecution swiftly took on various brutal forms:

the expulsion of Protestants from Paris, the massacre of the Waldensians in Savoy, refusal of burial, fresh dragonnades, children carried off, returning pastors hunted down and the penalty of death promised to any "caught making assemblies"— and actually carried out on six hundred of them.[16]

It is estimated that "of a million Huguenots, perhaps 200,000" fled to other countries.[17] Three hundred years after the event, the arrogance and inhumanity of this exercise of power is still a mind-boggling episode in the history of man's inhumanity to man.

It was more than a passing incident. The persecution of Protestants that followed the revocation of the Edict of Nantes continued well into the sixth decade of the eighteenth century. Under the laws of France Protestants continued to be outlaws and accordingly were still excluded from the holding of public office and were ineligible for the practice of law, medicine, or pharmacy. Other occupations for which they were considered to be disqualified were those of midwife, bookseller, goldsmith, and grocer. Only Catholic priests were authorized to perform the marriage service. Accordingly French Protestant wives were considered to be concubines, and their children were deemed to be illegitimate and, therefore, not qualified to inherit property. Protestant services were forbidden; men found at such services were to be sent away to the galleys for life; women so found were condemned to life imprisonment; and the officiating clergyman was subject to the death penalty.[18]

It is said that "these laws were not strictly enforced in or near Paris," and that "the severity of their enforcement varied with the distance," becoming more virulent as distance progressed to the south.[19]

Despite this appraisal, under Louis XV there were several outbreaks of persecution. In 1717 seventy-four Frenchmen caught in Protestant assemblage were sent to the galleys and the women were jailed. An edict of 1724 decreed death for Protestant preachers. "In 1749 the Parlement of Bordeaux ordered the separation of forty-six couples who had been married by Protestant rites. Children of parents who were suspected of Protestanism could be taken from them to be brought up in Catholic homes" and "we hear of a rich Huguenot spending 200,000 livres in bribing officials to let him keep his children." Between 1744 and 1752 some six hundred Protestants were imprisoned, and eight hundred others were subjected to various penalties. In 1752 the Protestant preacher Benezet, twenty-six years old, was hanged at Montpellier.[20]

Toulouse, in the deep south of France, was the very citadel of hatred against Protestants and the scene in 1761 of a case similar to the later Dreyfus affair. Something of the depth of religious animosity in Toulouse in 1761 can be judged by its continued celebration of an event that had occurred in 1562 during the Wars of Religion. At that time, the Catholics of Toulouse defeated the Protestants of Toulouse, three thousand of whom were condemned to death by the Toulouse Parlement. That happy occasion was thereafter commemorated annually in Toulouse with grateful ceremonies and a religious procession.[21]

In 1701, just as Toulouse was approaching the fervor of the bicentennial celebration of its 1562 victory, one of the sons of Jean Calas, a Protestant still living in Toulouse, committed suicide. The incident was not only tragic for Calas, but the timing was especially unfortunate; for in the heat of the city's religious celebration Calas was falsely accused of having murdered his son to prevent his conversion to Catholicism. On that specious charge he was tried, convicted, tortured, and put to death. Not satisfied with the punishment meted out to Jean Calas, all his property was confiscated by the state, his two daughters were sent to separate convents, and the rest of his family, humiliated and fearful, fled from Toulouse—his widow and one son going into hiding at Montauban and the other remaining son, Donat, escaping to Geneva.[22]

It was at that point that the great man of eighteenth-century France, the one and only François Marie Arouet Voltaire[23] (1694-

1778), became involved in the unhappy case of Jean Calas—an intervention that is pertinent here because it helps to clarify the character and significance of the philosophes. Hearing of the tragedy, Voltaire invited Donat to meet him at his estate, Les Délices, "just outside the gates of Geneva but within its jurisdiction."[24] After discussing the matter with Donat, Voltaire conducted his own investigation through friends and acquaintances and then, convinced that there had been a miscarriage of justice, launched a campaign to annul the conviction of Jean Calas and to obtain compensation for his family for the loss of their property.

In the course of that campaign he brought the rest of the Calas family to Paris so that they would be available for examination; engaged a lawyer to advise him about the legal technicalities of the case; wrote, published, and distributed pamphlets about the injustice that had been committed; appealed to other writers to "cry out for the Calas family and against fanaticism;"[25] appealed to influential friends among the clergy and the nobility to importune the king's ministers to order an investigation of the trial;[26] and solicited funds to help him bear the expenses of the campaign.[27]

As a result of these efforts the widow of Jean Calas and her daughters were given an audience by the king's ministers on March 26, 1763, which concluded with a verdict unanimously deciding that the trial should be investigated and ordering the delivery of all relevant documents by Toulouse. The authorities in Toulouse then resorted to a variety of excuses for delaying the transmission of the relevant papers. At that point Voltaire wrote what Durant has described as "his epochal Traité sur la tolérance."[28]

He concluded his "Treatise on Toleration" with a humanist address to the Deity in which he said, in part:

> Thou hast not given us hearts to hate, nor hands to kill one another. . . . May the trifling differences in the garments that cover our frail bodies, in the mode of expressing our . . . thoughts, in our ridiculous customs and imperfect laws . . . in a word, may the slightest variations that are found among the atoms called men not be used by us as signals of mutual hatred and persecution! . . . May all men remember that they are brothers.[29]

While it cannot be said that this plea influenced Louis XVI to issue an edict of toleration in 1787, or that it was a decisive influence in the final result in the Calas case, the fact is that on March 9, 1765, the King's Council "declared the condemnation of Jean Calas annulled and pronounced him innocent" and the king granted thirty thousand livres to the Calas family for the loss of their property.[30]

The point of this excursion into the life of Voltaire is that the Calas case and Voltaire's role in it epitomize the characteristics of those who achieved the distinction of the proud title of philosophe. The men in this select circle combined the qualities of intellectual originality, idealism, and worldly sophistication and practicality. In chronological order, Voltaire was the first, and probably the greatest, of the philosophes. The last of them was another great man and a distinguished philosophe as well—the Marquis de Condorcet (1743–1794), the central figure in this study, whose legacy to us, the *Sketch*, preserves the spirit of the Age of Enlightenment.

Between the birth of Voltaire in 1694 and the death of Condorcet one hundred years later, several other luminaries arrived upon the scene whose way of life and contributions to that bright age have earned for them acceptance in the special hall of fame reserved by history for philosophes. They include

Denis Diderot (1713-1784); Claude Adrian Helvétius (1715-1771); Jean Le Rond d'Alembert (1717-1783); Paul Henry Dietrich, Baron d'Holbach (1723-1789); and Anne Robert Jacques, Baron Turgot (1727-1781).[31]

When Baron d'Holbach died in 1789, Condorcet, as the last of the principal philosophes, was the only one left of that illustrious group to play an active part in the French Revolution. He alone among them had the opportunity of acting upon and experiencing the fruition of the philosophes' concepts regarding liberty, political rights, and equality. Only he was able to participate in the organization of a democratic society to replace the absolute monarchy. But because he survived them all, he alone among them suffered the indignity of death in prison, a victim of injustice aided and abetted by revolutionary fanaticism.

Notes

1. William H. Harris and Judith S. Levey, eds., *The New Columbia Encyclopedia* (New York: Columbia University Press, 1975), p. 1227.
2. See Robin Briggs, *Early Modern France 1560-1715* (Oxford: Oxford University Press, 1977), p. 96.
3. Robin Briggs, *Early Modern France 1560-1715*, p. 98.
4. Ibid., p. 98.
5. Pierre Goubert, *Louis XIV and the Twenty Million Frenchmen* (New York: Vintage Books, 1972), p. 61.
6. Ibid., p. 290.
7. Ibid., p. 64.
8. See *Bartlett's Familiar Quotations*, 13th (Centennial) ed. (Boston: Little, Brown & Co., 1955), p. 399b.
9. Ibid., p. 64.
10. William Doyle, *The Origins of the French Revolution*, student ed. (Oxford: Oxford University Press, 1984), p. 53.

11. Goubert, *Louis XIV and the Twenty Million Frenchmen*, p. 76.

12. Ibid., p. 159.

13. "(dragons = dragoons) repressive forces employed by the Government to terrorize and intimidate the Huguenots, before 1685"—Ibid., Appendix 2.

14. Goubert, *Louis XIV and the Twenty Million Frenchmen*, p. 91.

15. Ibid., p. 159.

16. Ibid., p. 160.

17. Ibid.

18. See Will and Ariel Durant, *The Age of Voltaire*, vol. 9 of *The Story of Civilization* (New York: Simon & Schuster, 1965), pp. 257 and 727.

19. Ibid., p. 727.

20. Ibid., p. 257.

21. Ibid., p. 727.

22. Ibid., p. 472.

23. "Voltaire" was an assumed name, adopted about 1717 or 1718, at the time he was imprisoned in the Bastille (ibid., pp. 35–36).

24. Ibid., p. 472.

25. Ibid., p. 730.

26. The influential friends included Cardinal de Bernis, the Duchess d'Enville, the Marquise de Necdai, the Duc de Villars, and the Duc de Richelieu. See ibid., p. 730.

27. The extent of Voltaire's influence can be judged by the fact that the contributors included the Queen of England, the Empress of Russia, and the King of Poland.

28. Ibid., p. 731.

29. Ibid., p. 732.

30. Ibid., p. 732. It is interesting to note that similar appeals were made to Voltaire in two other cases of fanatic persecution—the Sirven case and the La Barre case and that he responded with help in both of them. His efforts resulted in a reversal in the Sirvan case and in an amendment of the criminal code under which La Barre had been convicted and executed (ibid., pp. 732–36).

31. J. Salwyn Shapiro, in *Condorcet and the Rise of Liberalism* (New York: Octagon Books, 1963), pp. 28-29, divides the philosophes into three "ranks": In the "first rank" in his classification are Voltaire, Rousseau (1712-1778), Diderot, Montesquieu (1680-1755), and Turgot (1727-1781). He places in the "second rank" Condorcet, d'Alembert, Helvétius, d'Holbach, Abbé St. Pierre (1658-1743), Abbé Raynal (1713-1796), and Abbé Mably (1709-1785). In the "third rank," he names Baron von Grim (1723-1807), Marquis de Chastellux (1734-1788), and Abbé Morellet (1727-1819). The Abbé Raynal, Baron von Grim, and Abbé Morellet survived Condorcet, but as previously noted, did not achieve his stature or influence. For that reason he is generally considered to be entitled to the title of "the last philosophe."

3

Censorship and *Lettres de Cachet*

The twentieth century did not invent thought control. A French, seventeenth-century George Orwell might well have written the 1684 edition of *Nineteen Eighty-Four*. It was then, during the reign of the Absolute One—the Grand Monarch, Louis XIV— that censorship reached its apogee in France. The objective, of course, "was to keep from the public mind any idea that might disturb vested beliefs and powers."[1] In this exercise of royal authority the king had a staunch and powerful ally in the Catholic Church, the established religion of France. It claimed to be "the sole depository and sole authorized interpreter of divine truth, and therefore to have the right to suppress heresy."[2] As Cardinal Richelieu described it in his *Political Testament*, the technique of administering censorship was designed to inspire fear on the premise that "of all the forces capable of producing results in public affairs, fear . . . is the most effective principle."[3]

Accordingly royal permission to publish was granted only to manuscripts "guaranteed by official censors to contain nothing offensive to Church or state."[4] The king, the church, the Council of State, the Parlements, and the Sorbonne together were the guardians of correct thought. They formed a gamut against possible deviation by errant writers, and each of them could veto the printing or publication of a manuscript deemed to be offensive. If, by chance, a manuscript escaped the interdiction of this network of critics, the power to suppress could be invoked. The tainted manuscript would then be consigned to destruction by fire and, in addition, the misguided writer and his associates, the printer and the bookseller, would be summarily punished.

One of the prerogatives assumed by the king, as the absolute monarch over all he surveyed was the issuance of *lettres de cachet,* under the terms of which those who offended him, the church, or other pillars of French society could be incarcerated in the Bastille for indefinite periods without prior notice or an opportunity to be heard.[5] That was the image of the future that confronted the writer who dared to express doubt or dissent in sixteenth- and seventeenth-century France.

An effective method of censorship was the limitation of the number of licensed printers—a very valuable privilege to those fortunate enough to be chosen as authorized printers. Fifteen were appointed each year until 1667 and only nine thereafter in the succeeding twelve years.[6] Printers and booksellers who made the fatal mistake of participating in the publication or sale of books that did not have the seal of approval risked the loss of the license to print in the case of the printers and servitude in the galleys in the case of booksellers.[7]

This system of censorship was carried forward into the eighteenth century. An edict was issued in 1723, while Louis XV occupied the throne of France, providing that "no publishers or others may print or reprint anywhere in the kingdom, any books without having obtained permission in advance by letters sealed with the Great Seal."[8] In 1757, following an attempt to assassinate Louis XV, another "savage" edict was issued decreeing the death penalty for "all who shall be convicted of having written or printed any works intended to attack religion, to assail the royal authority, or to disturb the tranquility of the realm."[9]

Despite these barriers, people continued to think their own thoughts, and intrepid characters, braving the dangerous rapids ahead, even dared to express them in writing. The hovering presence of the censors and the dire consequence of unapproved publication, however, necessitated resort to the use of stratagems designed to evade or deceive the censors' supervision. The subterfuges designed by writers and printers were many and sometimes clever. Among them were:

> secret printing presses, as in the case of the *Encyclopédie;* anonymous authorship, as in the case of Voltaire's many pamphlets against the church; pretended authorship, as in the case of Diderot's *Letters on the Blind* which pretended to explain the work of an Englishman; imaginary letters of travelers, a common device, the most notable being Montesquieu's *Persian Letters,* and imaginary translations of foreign books, a method often resorted to by d'Holbach.[10]

The bootlegging of proscribed books in the eighteenth century was also a common practice, not unlike the bootlegging of liquor during the period of prohibition under the Eighteenth Amendment to the Constitution.[11] The two "prohibitions" were comparable in that both involved "spies, raids and bribery of police."[12]

In some ways the censorship experienced by French intellectuals at this time was also comparable to that imposed on writers and artists living under the Soviet system in our century. But there was a legal method of avoiding censorship in prerevolutionary France which was not available to twentieth-century

Russian and Eastern-bloc intellectuals. The former could voluntarily leave France to carry on their work in a foreign country, such as Holland, free from the impediment of censorship. That is precisely what Pierre Bayle (1647–1706) did, of whom more later.

In assessing the effect of censorship and *lettres de cachet* upon the philosophes it should be noted that several of them took risks and became the victims of oppression.

Voltaire's first encounter with censorship and *lettres de cachet* occurred on May 16, 1717, when, oddly enough, he was summarily arrested and jailed in the Bastille based on a bit of poetry regarding Louis XIV and Mme. de Maintenon, which he did not write. Nevertheless, for an offense he didn't commit and without notice or an opportunity to be heard, he was imprisoned in the Bastille for nearly a year. When he was released on April 11, 1718, he was forbidden to stay in Paris. That restriction was not lifted until October 12, 1718.[13]

Eight years later Voltaire became involved in a feud with an arrogant member of the nobility, the Chevalier de Rohan-Chabot. The feud originated with an impudent remark by the Chevalier, to which Voltaire responded in a way that did not please the Chevalier's tender sensibilities. To soothe his ruffled feelings the Chevalier engaged six men to administer a beating of Voltaire under his supervision. When Voltaire recovered he challenged the Chevalier to a duel. Thereupon Voltaire was arrested, pursuant to royal order, and was again imprisoned in the Bastille. This time he remained in the Bastille for a brief period of fifteen days. His quick release, however, was subject to the condition of his exile in England. There he remained for two years from 1726 to 1728.[14]

As it happened Voltaire's exile and sojourn in England for two years had a fortuitous result. It familiarized him with English government, politics, literature, and science, and led to the writing of an influential commentary pointing up the marked differences between France and England in matters of religious tolerance and political and intellectual freedom—a contrast not favorable to France. The commentary took the form of twenty-four letters addressed by Voltaire to a friend, Nicholas Claude Thieriot (1696–1772). The letters, Voltaire's "first contribution to the Enlightenment,"[15] were published in 1733 and 1734, nine years before the birth of Condorcet.

A sentence or two, taken from the letters, will convey a sense of their critical character regarding the philosophy and attitude of French authority with respect to religion and human rights. On religion, he said of England, "This is a land of sects. An Englishman, like a free man, goes to heaven by whatever route he chooses."[16] On government he said, "Only the English have managed to regulate the power of kings by resisting them."[17] On the subject of the status of people he said:

> The English Constitution has, in fact, arrived at the point of excellence, in consequence of which all men are restored to those natural rights which in nearly all monarchies they are deprived of. Those rights are entire liberty of person and property; freedom of the press; the right of being tried in all cases by a jury of independent men; the right of being tried only according to the strict letter of the law; the right of every man to profess, unmolested, what religion he chooses.[18]

Voltaire tried to get the French Government to approve the publication of the letters but, as might be expected, it was not the kind of literature that appealed to the critical mind of censors, intent upon protecting the public mind from troubling thoughts. Then Voltaire resorted to underground printing. He warned the printer, however, not to circulate any copies of this printing until he received further instructions. But a private publisher secured a copy and "printed a large edition without Voltaire's knowledge."[19]

The customary French assault upon independent thinking and self-expression then moved into action. The printer was sent to the Bastille and a *lettre de cachet* was issued for the arrest of Voltaire. Voltaire's friends had already warned him of his impending arrest and he fled before the police could seize him.

Ultimately, through the influence of titled friends, a deal was struck with the Keeper of the Seals, who agreed to rescind the order of arrest if Voltaire would disclaim authorship of the Letters. To that he agreed and the order of arrest was rescinded, subject to the further condition that Voltaire would "remain at a respectful distance from Paris."[20] For ten happy years he then retired to the chateau of Mme. du Chatelet at Cirey in Champagne "as the paying guest of his mistress and her husband."[21] That tenth year occurred in 1744, one year after the birth of Condorcet.

The sojourn at Cirey was not the last time that Voltaire was denied access to Paris, nor was his English visit the only occasion when he had to seek asylum in another country. Voltaire was to run afoul of French censorship many times in his long career.[22] The same was true of several of the other philosophes.

In 1758 Helvétius' book *De l'Esprit* (On intelligence) was published, surprisingly, with the approval of the king. The censor, Jean Pierre Tercier, reported that he had found "nothing in it which in my judgment ought to prevent its publication."[23] Despite that judgment, the advocate general of the Paris parliament expressed a markedly different opinion—that the book contained "a mass of heresies."[24] The Council of State thereupon revoked the privilege to print. To avoid arrest and incarceration in the Bastille, Helvétius issued a retraction. When this was held to be inadequate, Helvétius further humiliated himself by signing an apology so abject that Grimm said, "One would not have been astonished to see a man take refuge with the Hottentots rather than put his name to such avowals."[25] While resort to refuge with the Hottentots might have been a more courageous couse of action, the apology together with the intercession of his wife at Versailles served the purpose of earning the more moderate sentence of confinement to his estate for two years. Tercier's failure to spot the "heresy" in *De l'Esprit* earned for the censor the loss of his position.[26]

Censorship and the indignity of the *lettres de cachet* were also suffered by the philosophe Denis Diderot (1713–1784). The first of his encounters with censorship occurred in 1749 in connection with the publication of his *Lettres sur les aveugles a l'usage de ceux qui voient* (Letters on the blind for the use of those who see). It was a book in which Diderot, to evade censorship, pretended that he was quoting from a work by a nonexistent person named William Inchliff, concerning the life of a blind professor, a Dr. Nicholas Saunderson. The book contained statements not consistent with the point of view approved by the establishment on the subject of religion. Despite the device used by Diderot to avoid censorship, he was arrested and incarcerated in the fortress of Vincenne on the outskirts of Paris, pursuant to a *lettre de cachet.* There he remained for three and a half months from August to November 1749.

While Diderot was a talented dramatist and novelist, the work that places him in the first rank of the philosophes was his editorship of the *Encyclopédie,* the centerpiece of the intellectual development of eighteenth-century France, a work that exercised great influence on the direction of Enlightenment thought just as Condorcet's *Sketch* was its end piece and has been its enduring testament. In 1747, when Condorcet was four years old, Diderot was engaged to be the editor-in-chief of the *Encyclopédie,* along with the noted mathematician d'Alembert who became, in effect, its scientific editor. Among its one hundred contributors were some of the most important intellectuals of the Enlightenment including Voltaire, Montesquieu, Rousseau, Helvétius, d'Holbach, Condorcet, Turgot, and, of course, Diderot and d'Alembert.

The *Encyclopédie,* under the direction of Diderot and d'Alembert, was both a compendium of knowledge and an instrument of propaganda, explaining and promoting the ideas of the Enlightenment such as liberty, equality, rights, reason, government, tolerance, and freedom from superstition and fixed theological assumptions. The multivolume work was critical of the established order, represented by state and church, particularly its intolerance, its orthodoxy, and its adherence to outmoded concepts of human rights.

Conscious of the problem of censorship a serious effort was made to present controversial ideas in ways designed to disarm censors. Nevertheless, the *Encyclopédie* had to struggle with censorship more than once in its harried life, primarily because of that recurrent nemesis of human relations—religion.

"Volume I [published in 1751] was not visibly antireligious."[27] Yet "Jean François Boyer, former bishop of Mirepoix, complained to the King that the authors had deceived the censors."[28] When Volume II was published in 1752, the archbishop of Paris, Christophe de Beaumont, "condemned the *Encyclopédie* as a subtle attack upon religion."[29] That condemnation was followed by a decree of the Council of State forbidding any further sale or publication of the work on the ground that it was a "revolt against God, the royal authority and a corruption of morals" and on that score it was said that "the authors of this dictionary . . . must shortly be put to death."[30] Although Diderot was not executed, or even arrested, nearly all of the materials he had gathered for the *Encyclopédie* were seized by the government.

Some months after the decree of the Council of State was issued, publication of additional volumes was permitted as the result of the intercession of influential friends including Mme. de Pompadour, but, to appease the clergy, it was agreed that "all future volumes should be censored by three theologians chosen by ex-bishop Boyer."[31] Volumes III to VI, published between 1753 and 1756, were all subjected to strict censorship in accordance with the directive that followed the publication of Volume II. Volume VII, published in 1757, inspired a particularly difficult encounter with censorship, an encounter so bruising in its effect that it nearly terminated the entire project. It came about as a consequence of an attempt to assassinate the king, who thereupon revived a law that "condemned to death the authors, publishers and sellers of books that attacked religion or disturbed the state."[32] Although not executed, several writers were then imprisoned.

This sequence of events so frightened the editors and contributors of the *Encylopédie* that its work came to a standstill; D'Alembert resigned; Turgot, Marmontel, Duclos, and Morellet refused to contribute additional articles; and Rousseau in a letter to d'Alembert gave public notice of the termination of his relations with the philosophes and, in addition, refused any further association with the *Encyclopédie*.

There were additional blows: The bishops of France in a presentation to the king urged him to terminate the "tacit permission" that permitted publication of the *Encyclopédie* in France. The king's attorney, de Fleury, cautioned the Paris parliament that "there is a project formed, a society organized, to propagate materialism, to destroy religion, to inspire a spirit of independence, and to nourish the corruption of morals."[33] Two months later, in March 1759, "an order of the Council of State completely outlawed the *Encyclopédie* and directed that no new volumes were to be printed and that no existing volumes were to be sold on the ground that "the advantages to be derived from a work of this sort . . . can never compensate for the irreparable damage that result from it in regard to morality and religion."[34]

Voltaire counseled Diderot to give up. But he was made of sterner stuff. He determined to carry on in the hope that the ban would be rescinded or that he would have the remaining volumes printed abroad. Nevertheless he, too, left Paris for a time, burdened with "a melancholy soul."[35]

Time is sometimes a healer of melancholy souls, and as Diderot had hoped the turmoil, both in his soul and in society, did subside. D'Alembert offered to resume his responsibility of editing the mathematical articles, an offer that was accepted; Voltaire, too, rejoined, and the production of the *Encyclopédie* continued. The last of twenty-eight volumes was published in 1772, twenty-one years after the publication of Volume I, followed by the publication of a five-volume supplement and a two-volume index between 1776 and 1780. Diderot was asked to edit the supplement and index, but he was too tired to undertake that job. As the Durants have put it, "The most important publishing enterprise of the century had consumed him, but had made him as immortal as the vicissitudes of civilization will permit."[36]

Notes

1. Will and Ariel Durant, *The Age of Voltaire,* vol. 9 of *The Story of Civilization* (New York: Simon & Schuster, 1965), p. 494.

2. Ibid., p. 494.

3. Henry B. Hill, trans., *The Political Testament of Cardinal Richelieu* (Madison: The University of Wisconsin Press, 1981), p. 118.

4. W. and A. Durant, *The Age of Voltaire,* p. 324.

5. See J. Salwyn Shapiro, *Condorcet and the Rise of Liberalism* (New York: Octagon Books, 1963), p. 40.

6. Pierre Goubert, *Louis XIV and the Twenty Million Frenchmen* (New York: Vintage Books, 1972), p. 94.

7. See Shapiro, *Condorcet and the Rise of Liberalism*, p. 40.

8. W. and A. Durant, *The Age of Voltaire*, p. 496.

9. Ibid., p. 496.

10. Shapiro, *Condorcet and the Rise of Liberalism*, p. 43.

11. Ibid., p. 43. The prohibition amendment, adopted in 1919, was repealed by the Twenty-first Amendment, adopted in 1933.

12. Ibid., p. 43.

13. See W. and A. Durant, *The Age of Voltaire*, pp. 34-36.

14. Ibid., p. 41.

15. Ibid., p. 366.

16. Ibid., p. 368.

17. Ibid.

18. Ibid.

19. Ibid., p. 366.

20. Ibid., p. 371.

21. Ibid.

22. In late 1754 or early 1755 Voltaire left France and established a home at Les Délices near Geneva where he remained until 1758 because of the objection of Louis XV to his presence in Paris following the publication of an abridged edition of Voltaire's *Essai sur l'histoire générale*. From 1758 to 1778, Voltaire's home was at Ferney, just three and a half miles from the Swiss Border.

Among Voltaire's books that were denied the royal privilege or from which the royal privilege was withdrawn were his *Histoire de Charles XII, roi de Suede* (1730-1731) and *Elements de la philosophie de Newton* (1738). See W. and A. Durant, *The Age of Voltaire*, pp. 362 and 375.

23. Ibid., p. 681.

24. Ibid.

25. Ibid.

26. It is an interesting comment about censorship that as a result of this "fuss over an omelet," as Voltaire called it, *De l'Esprit* became a very widely read book. "Twenty editions appeared in French within six months and it was soon translated into English and German" (ibid., p. 682).

27. Ibid., p. 637.
28. Ibid., p. 638.
29. Ibid., p. 639.
30. Ibid., p. 640.
31. Ibid., p. 639.
32. Ibid., p. 641.
33. Ibid., p. 642.
34. Ibid.
35. Ibid., p. 643.
36. Ibid., p. 644.

Part Two

Intellectual Influences

4

Skepticism—Montaigne, Descartes, and Bayle

Skepticism, the expression of doubt, had its occasional exponents in France in the sixteenth and seventeenth centuries despite the oppressive weight of the authority of state and church, which were ever intent upon maintaining obedience in conduct and conformity in thought.[1] The principal torchbearers of sixteenth- and seventeenth-century independence in thinking, in the order in which they appeared upon the scene, were Michel Eyquem de Montaigne (1533-1592), René Descartes (1596-1650), and Pierre Bayle (1647-1706).

Montaigne's most memorable contribution to the literature of skepticism is a question—"What do I know?"[2] It was written in 1580 in an essay bearing the title "Apology for Raymond Sebond."[3] Raymond Sebond was a professor of theology, medicine, and philosophy at Toulouse in southern France around 1480. He wrote a book in 1484 entitled *Natural Theology*, which impressed Montaigne's father and, at his request, Montaigne translated it. Its premise interested Montaigne, who thereupon used it as the vehicle for the expression of his skeptical views about reason and knowledge.

As stated by Montaigne, Sebond's purpose in writing *Natural Theology* was "bold and courageous, for he undertakes by human and natural reasons to establish and prove against the atheists all the articles of the Christian religion."[4] Montaigne's defense of Sebond's thesis is brief and perfunctory. In fact it is used as the point of departure for the expression of what Will and Ariel Durant have said is "perhaps the most thoroughgoing exposition of skepticism in modern literature."[5]

Far from agreeing with Sebond about the relation between reason and religion, Montaigne says almost at the outset of his essay, "It is faith alone that embraces vividly and surely the high mysteries of our religion."[6] At a later point in his essay, Montaigne discounts reason as a factor in religious belief, saying, "It is not by reasoning or by our understanding that we have received our religion; it is by external authority and command"[7]

While the thrust of his essay on Raymond Sebond is that faith, not reason, is the basis for religious belief, Montaigne used the occasion of that essay to express his reservation concerning the reliability of knowledge acquired through reason on subjects other than religion. The tenor of his doubts about the reliability of such knowledge is expressed in a statement and an illustration.

The statement, in part, is "that of all vanities, the vainest is man, that the man who is presumptuous of his knowledge does not yet know what knowledge is; and that man, who is nothing, if he thinks he is something, seduces and deceives himself."[8]

The illustration—serious in purpose and yet amusing in its statement—expresses his analysis of the human relationship with the world of animals: "How does he know," Montaigne asks, "by the force of his intelligence, the secret internal stirring of animals? By what comparison between them and us does he infer the stupidity that he attributes to them? When I play with my cat, who knows if I am not a pastime to her more than she is to me?"[9]

The guide to Montaigne's philosophy is anchored in the question "What do I know?"—words, he says, that "I wear as a motto, inscribed over a pair of scales."[10] The motto was also "engraved on his seal and inscribed on his library ceiling."[11]

The elevation of that question to the status of his life's motto and its use in an essay about reason and religious belief underscores Montaigne's conviction that it is desirable to be constantly reminded of the need for modesty in the assertion of certainty about the truth of religious beliefs. It can also be construed as a continuing challenge to the pretensions of those who are sure that they are the possessors of truth. This challenge applies especially to those who claim to possess religious truth, but the motto can also be read as a reminder that knowledge acquired through the process of reason is not necessarily infallible.

If, as the Durants have said, "Montaigne was the grandfather, as Bayle was the father of the Enligtenment,"[12] then René Descartes should also be ranked in some close familial relationship to the Enlightenment; for this thinker, who has exercised a major influence on modern philosophy, was an immediate progenitor of the germ of ideas that flowered in the eighteenth century.

Descartes, prompted by his desire for bedrock upon which to build his world of certainty, engaged himself in a quest for knowledge that could not be doubted. He said,

> I did not wish to imitate the skeptics, who doubted only for the sake of doubting, and intended to remain always irresolute.

On the contrary, my whole purpose was to achieve greater certainty and to reject the loose earth and sand in favor of rock and clay.[13]

And so, in the pursuit of that goal he set aside:

anything which admits of the slightest doubt . . . just as if I had found it to be wholly false; and I will proceed in this way until I recognize something certain, or if nothing else, until I at least recognize for certain that there is no certainty.[14]

The forbidding prospect that there is nothing in this world that is certain was averted because Descartes discovered the "rock and clay" of certainty in the fact of his own existence, a certainty triumphantly proclaimed in "the most famous sentence in philosophy"—"I think, therefore I am."[15] D'Alembert summed up the influence of Descartes upon the Enlightenment in his introduction to Volume I of the *Encyclopédie,* entitled "Discours Préliminaire":

Descartes at least dared to show to alert minds how to free themselves from the yoke of scholasticism, opinion, authority— in a word from prejudice and barbarism; and by this revolt of which we today gather the fruits, he rendered to philosophy a service perhaps more difficult than all those that it owes to his renowned successors. . . . If he finished by thinking to explain everything he at least began by doubting all.[16]

Pierre Bayle's principal contribution to the eighteenth-century philosophes was his two-volume *Dictionnaire historique et critique.* It was predominantly a work of criticism and skepticism, a kind of ultimate expression of doubt and disbelief in all the accepted verities and pieties, religious, social, and political, which were promoted and protected by the authority of church and state. In the *Encyclopedia of Philosophy* Bayle is described as opposed to "everything that is said and everything that is done."[17] The statement may sound like hyperbole, but it is warranted by the depth of Bayle's skepticism.

The *Dictionnaire* was published between 1695 and 1697, on the eve of the eighteenth century and, for that reason, it exercised an effect upon the Enlightenment that was both more immediate and profound than the work of Montaigne and Descartes. Pierre Goubert, in describing the influence of Bayle and his work, calls the *Dictionnaire* "intellectual dynamite" and says that "his famous *Dictionnaire*" contained "all the seeds of Voltaire."[18] Voltaire called it "the arsenal of the Enlightenment."[19] "Thomas Jefferson recommended the *Dictionary* as one of the hundred basic books with which to start the Congressional Library."[20]

While he considered most human mental efforts to be "big with contradictions and absurdity"[21] and his reactions to them were generally negative, there were some subjects on which he was forcefully positive. One of those subjects was the relationship between religious belief and moral behavior. He has been described as "a moralist," a term used to describe one who believes that there is "a natural equity" in man and that "conscience is the supreme rule in life."[22] In modern philosophical parlance he might be classified as an "intuitionist," because he rejected the authoritarian Judaeo-Christian subscription to moral standards derived from divine revelation. In that vein, for example, the *Dictionnaire* discusses the independence of morality from religion, the immorality of great figures in the Old Testament, the irrationality of aspects of Christianity, and the "then scandalous thesis that a society of atheists could be moral and a society of Christians immoral."[23]

Total religious tolerance was another aspect of Bayle's positive point of view. This attitude was derived from his observation of differences in religious beliefs, the divisive conflicts between French Catholics and French Protestants and, undoubtedly, his own bitter personal memories as a result of that conflict. Both his father and his brother were Calvinists who died in France as victims of religious intolerance.

In politics, Bayle was a proponent of the sovereignty of the political state, so long as the entire social structure was "held together not by religion but by common secular interests."[24] According to Robin Briggs, Bayle's writings "constituted a subtle but deadly assault on the values by which Louis XIV lived."[25]

Although his critics insisted that he was an unbeliever, Bayle "always claimed to be a Calvinist Christian."[26] "He persisted in belonging to" the French Reformed Church, "attending it and proclaiming his sincere adherence to it," regardless of the denunciations of his enemies. His last message to a friend as he knew his life was ending was "I am dying as a Christian philosopher, convinced of and pierced by the bounties and mercy of God."[27]

It is surprising that Montaigne, Descartes, and Bayle appear to have escaped the twin dragons of censorship and *lettres de cachet,* despite their expressions of doubt, which challenged those guardians of truth who brooked no doubts. One explanation in the cases of Descartes and Bayle is that both published their views within the safe haven of a tolerant foreign country—Holland. Descartes moved to Holland in 1628, when he was thirty-two, and remained there for twenty-one years, except for occasional visits to France. In 1649, he went to Sweden at the invitation of Queen Christina and there he died on February 11, 1650, a victim of the rigors of Swedish life and winters. Bayle exiled himself from France in 1681, settling in Rotterdam, where he lived and worked for most of the rest of his life until his death in 1706.

Montaigne, who remained in France and published his

writings there, presents a different case. Perhaps, he escaped censure because censorship was less rigorous in the sixteenth century than it was in the seventeenth century during the reign of Louis XIV. But, more likely, Montaigne, like other skeptics of the sixteenth and seventeenth centuries, gave the appearance of being a conformist. He, like "Bathsheba, bowed and did obeisance unto the" Catholic Church.

In 1580, for example, on a tour of Europe, shortly after the first publication of the *Essays,* his "greatest event was a visit to Gregory XIII" and "like any son of the Church" he "knelt to kiss the papal shoe."[28] Then "he journeyed across Italy to the shrine of the Virgin at Loreto and dedicated a votive tablet to her."[29]

In spite of these public displays of devotion, there is a certain lack of clarity about Montaigne's religious convictions. Students of his life have been puzzled and doubtful about them because they suspect a tendency to dissemble as a protective measure. Sainte-Beuve, for example, judged the *Apology for Raymond Sebond* to be "a tongue-in-the-cheek argument for unbelief."[30] A modern editor of Montaigne's *Essays* describes his religious views as that of "a mere conforming Catholicism."[31]

Summing up Montaigne's views on religion, Richard Popkin, in his article on "Skepticism in Modern Thought" in the *Dictionary of the History of Ideas,* says, "Whether Montaigne was a genuine Christian, or whether he was a covert nonbeliever, is still extremely difficult to determine."[32] The Durants' conclusion is that Montaigne "remained a Catholic long after he ceased to be a Christian."[33]

Nevertheless, despite the ambivalence of later analysts about his convictions, his contemporaries accepted his exposition of his thoughts about religion as a measure of support for theirs. "By and large Montaigne's generalized skepticism and his fideism were accepted by the counter-reformers in France as a basis for rebutting the new dogmas of Protestantism and for accepting the traditional religion on faith."[34]

I think that a case can be made for the opinion that Montaigne was religious in the fundamental sense of belief in the existence of God as the Supreme Being, without the embellishments and rituals that countless generations have embroidered around that belief. It was a simple belief, based on faith, as stated in the concluding words of the *Apology for Raymond Sebond:*

> Nor can man raise himself above himself and humanity for he can see only with his own eyes, and seize only with his own grasp.
>
> He will rise, if God by exception lends him a hand; he will rise by abandoning and renouncing his own means, and letting himself be raised and uplifted by purely celestial means.
>
> It is for our Christian faith, not for his stoical virtue, to aspire to that divine and miraculous metamorphosis.[35]

This philosophy, which combined skepticism and religious belief on the basis of faith, was carried forward by his disciple, friend, and heir—Pierre Charron. Charron was born in Paris in 1544, a member of a family remarkable for the fact that it numbered twenty-five. He received a law degree from the University of Montpellier in 1571, but became a priest rather than a lawyer, and, as it happened, a very successful one, both as a preacher and as a theological adviser and teacher.

He met Montaigne in the 1580s in Bordeaux and soon became both his close friend and disciple. After Montaigne's death in 1592 he had a career as a prolific and popular writer. One of his treatises—*De la Sagesse*, published in 1601, just two years before his death—was influential in promulgating the skeptical point of view developed by Montaigne. It is notable principally for the idea that "the complete skeptic will never be a heretic, since if he has no opinions, he cannot have the wrong ones."[36] That leads to the conclusion that since skepticism requires the rejection of all doubtful opinions, the mind, naked and blank, is ready to receive the divine revelation on faith alone. Faith is the cornerstone of religious belief in this analysis. Charron's work and his clerical career have been summed up to suggest that "he was a sincere fideist, who saw skepticism as a means of destroying the enemies of the true faith while preparing the soul for salvation."[37]

It is noteworthy, therefore, that the sixteenth- and seventeenth-century skeptics did not carry their skepticism to the alternative ultimate logic of heresy. They accepted the premise of "two truths," a formulation attributed to Pierre Gassendi (1592–1655). Gassendi, at twenty-five a professor of philosophy at the University of Aix, took holy orders and became a canon and provost of the cathedral at Digne. "Throughout his life he professed the doctrine of the 'two truths'—that the conclusions apparently compelled by reason could be accepted in philosophy, while in religion one might still follow the orthodox faith and ritual as an obedient son of the Church."[38] That path, as we have seen, was followed even by the arch skeptic Pierre Bayle.

We have looked at some of the bright lights of intellectual history in this brief review of skepticism in the sixteenth and seventeenth centuries. Before concluding, we should consider some of the lesser luminaries who also represented the spirit of the liberated mind. Among them were Francisco Sanches (1550–1623), a distant cousin of Montaigne; François de la Motte le Vayer (1588–1672), a teacher of the dauphin; Gabriel Naudé (1600–1653), secretary to cardinal Mazarin; Guy Patin (1602–1672), Rector of the Sorbonne; and Theophile de Viau, a libertine poet who was tried for blasphemy in 1625.

Perhaps the most interesting of the minor pioneers of critial thinking, who undertook the hazardous experiment of expressing independent thought, was a French courtier, Isaac La Payrère. In some ways, he was a predecessor of Ernest Renan in the critical study of the Bible. Based on evidence derived from explorations of the New World, China, and Greenland, he reached the radical conclusion that the Bible does not present an accurate account of the origin of the human race and that Adam was not the first man. While self-preservation might have counseled him to keep that discovery to himself, he was unable to resist the demand for self-expression. In 1655 he published his theory about origins in a book entitled *Prae-Adamitae* (Man before Adam). Retribution for this heresy was swiftly administered: La Peyrère's book was promptly suppressed and the author was jailed.

Subsequently, in order to restore his status as a respected member of seventeenth-century society, he converted from Calvinism to Catholicism, apologized to the pope, and retired to the haven of an Oratorian Order.[39] There his mind continued to function and theorize in safety.

The career of Isaac La Peyrère points to one of the circumstances that led bright and active minds to be skeptical about some of the points of view considered by the authority of church and state to be sacrosanct and unquestionable. At this time, many of the assumptions and beliefs that had been inherited from the Middle Ages were being challenged, not only by the discoveries of the sixteenth-century explorers, but by the rediscovery of Greek and Roman civilization and the upheaval in religious thinking caused by the Reformation. The probing, the questioning, and the assaults by the contesting Catholic and Protestant opponents inevitably revealed the uncertainties and even the deficiencies in each side's beliefs.

Skepticism and ultimately the revolt against absolutism in all its forms in the later eighteenth century had its roots in the doubts, questions, and arguments posed by sixteenth- and seventeenth-century skeptics.

Notes

1. "Modern skepticism, which played a great role in the development of modern thought, entered the intellectual arena in the sixteenth century." *Dictionary of the History of Ideas* (New York: Charles Scribner's Sons, 1973), vol. 4, p. 241.

2. *Que sais-je?*

3. For a translation of this essay see Donald M. Frame, trans. and ed., *Selections from the Essays of Montaigne* (Crofts Classics, 1969), pp. 50–71, hereafter referred to as the "Frame translation."

4. Frame translation, p. 54.

5. Will and Ariel Durant, *The Age of Reason Begins*, vol. 7 of *The Story of Civilization* (New York: Simon and Schuster, 1961), p. 407.

6. Frame translation, p. 61.

7. Ibid.

8. Ibid., p. 59.

9. Ibid., p. 60. Interestingly enough, *Newsweek* magazine's cover story, in its May 23, 1988, issue is entitled "How Smart Are Animals?" with the subtitle "They Know More Than You Think."

10. Ibid., p. 63.

11. W. and A. Durant, *The Age of Reason Begins*, p. 408.

12. Ibid., p. 414.

13. *Discours de la methode*, written in 1629 and published in 1637. See translation by Laurence J. Lafleur (New York: Macmillan, 1960), p. 18.

14. *Meditations on First Philosophy*, trans. John Cottingham (Cambridge: Cambridge University Press), p. 15. *Meditations* was first pub-

lished in 1641. The same thought is expressed in slightly different language in the *Discourse on Method*, Lafleur translation, p. 20.

15. *Je pense, donc je suis*, or in Latin, *Cogito, ergo sum*. This dictum appears in the *Discours de la méthode*. (See Lafleur translation, p. 21.) It is an interesting aspect of skepticism that the dyed-in-the-wool skeptic is unwilling to accept even "I think, therefore I am" as a true proposition. Daniel Huet's *Censura Philosophica Cartesiana* (1698) took the position that Descartes' fundamental proposition stands for no more than "I may have thought, therefore perhaps I may be."

16. See Will and Ariel Durant, *The Age of Voltaire*, vol. 9 of *The Story of Civilization* (New York: Simon and Schuster, 1965), p. 637.

17. Paul Edwards, ed., *Encyclopedia of Philosophy* (New York: Free Press, 1973), vol. 7, p. 454.

18. Pierre Goubert, *Louis XIV and the Twenty Million Frenchmen*, trans. Anne Carter (New York: Vintage Books, 1972), p. 189.

19. *Dictionary of the History of Ideas*, vol. 4, p. 247.

20. P. Edwards, ed., *Encyclopedia of Philosophy*, vol. 1, p. 259.

21. Ibid., p. 259.

22. Alfred Cobban, *A History of Modern France* (New York: Penguin Books, 1961), p. 81.

23. P. Edwards, ed., *Encyclopedia of Philosophy*, vol. 1, p. 259.

24. Alfred Cobban, *A History of Modern France*, vol. 1, p. 84.

25. Robin Briggs, *Early Modern France 1560-1715* (Oxford: Oxford University Press, 1977), p. 164.

26. P. Edwards, ed., *The Encyclopedia of Philosophy*, vol. 1, p. 260.

27. Ibid., p. 261.

28. W. and A. Durant, *The Age of Reason Begins*, p. 407. On this visit Montaigne was gently chided by the Holy Office that "some passages smelled of heresy." In 1676 the *Essays* were placed on the Index.

29. Ibid., p. 407.

30. Ibid.

31. Montaigne, *Essays*, ed. J. M. Cohen, Introduction, (New York: Penguin Books, 1959), p. 16.

32. Richard H. Popkin in *Dictionary of the History of Ideas*, vol.

4, p. 243.

33. W. and A. Durant, *The Age of Reason Begins*, p. 410.

34. R. H. Popkins in *Dictionary of the History of Ideas*, vol. 4, p. 243.

35. Frame Translation, p. 71.

36. Richard H. Popkin in *Encyclopedia of Philosophy*, ed. P. Edwards, vol. 2, p. 82.

37. Ibid.

38. W. and A. Durant, *The Age of Reason Begins*, p. 635.

39. An Oratorio is a religious society of secular priests who live in religious communities but do not take vows.

5

Science and Reason—
Newton and Locke

From the perspective of the twentieth century, it is apparent that seeds of doubt about long-established beliefs were sown by the adventurous independent thinkers of the Enlightenment in the sixteenth and seventeenth centuries. The inquisitorial frame of mind characteristic of the monarchy and the church in France, which was devoted to the limitation and containment of unorthodox thought, was from time to time quietly but effectively challenged by new ideas from abroad and, sometimes more subtly, at home. Although the net effect of sixteenth- and seventeenth-century skepticism might have been negative—questioning and doubting rather than affirming—there were other influences at work during the same period that contributed to the formation of the very positive point of view of the eighteenth-century philosophes.

Two towering seventeenth-century English personalities who had a particularly direct and positive influence upon the thinking of French philosophes a century later were Sir Isaac Newton and John Locke.

Newton

Isaac Newton possessed one of the great minds in the history of the human race. It is interesting to note, as a striking bit of trivia, that Newton was born in 1642, the same year that marked the death of a predecessor genius, Galileo Galilei, whose thinking in some respects foreshadowed Newton's.[1] One can only speculate, with a high degree of awe, upon the extraordinary combination of neurons, dendrites, and synapses in Newton's brain: Within a period of about eighteen months, between his twenty-second and twenty-fourth birthdays, he discovered nothing less than the law of universal gravitation and invented the tool of calculus.[2]

That was approximately the period between 1664 and 1666 when the University of Cambridge was closed as a result of the plague. It was then that Newton retired to his home town of Woolsthorpe in Lincolnshire and there formulated in mathematical terms, among other things, the findings establishing that terrestrial and celestial motions conform to precisely the same laws. His development of the concept of universal gravitation provided "an explanation both of falling bodies on the earth and the motion of planets, comets and other bodies in the heavens."[3]

Oddly enough, it was not until twenty-one years later that Newton published his findings about gravitation, a delay that probably occurred because he was excessively sensitive to criticism. In any event the plunge was finally taken. He exposed himself to the slings and arrows of public scrutiny in 1687 with the publication of one of the great milestones of the written word, entitled *Philosophiae Naturalis Principia Mathematia* (Mathematical principles of natural philosophy), more familiarly known as *Principia*.

Newton did not pretend to know or explain the cause of

gravitation. In the spirit of scientific restraint he limited his exposition to the how, not the why. As he said, in part, in the conclusion of the second edition of the *Principia*:

> Hitherto we have explained the phenomena of the heavens and of our sea by the power of gravity, but have not yet assigned the cause of this power. . . . To us it is enough that gravity does really exist and act according to the laws which we have explained, and abundantly serves to account for all the motions of the celestial bodies and of our sea. . . . We are to admit no more causes of natural things than such as are both true and sufficient to explain their appearances. Therefore, to the same natural effects we must, as far as possible, assign the same causes. . . . We must, in consequence of this rule, universally allow, that all bodies are endowed with a principle of mutual gravitation.[4]

Newton need not have feared the outcome of the publication of the *Principia*. Recognized and accepted immediately as a great contribution to human knowledge, it had an immense impact both at home and abroad, not only in terms of its remarkable scientific revelations but also because of the tremendous impetus it gave to confidence in the power and efficacy of reason, which it amply demonstrated. The persuasive evidence furnished by the *Principia* of a rational universe governed by mathematical laws supported and encouraged the devotion to the life of reason that dominated the Age of Enlightenment.

Voltaire, it will be recalled, was exiled to England and remained there for two years from 1726 to 1728. During those two years he met many of the English great, familiarized himself with English literature and government, and, of more importance in this context, he also became acquainted with Newton's work.

That acquaintance made him a disciple, a teacher, and an ardent advocate of Newton's portrayal of the laws governing the operations of the universe. As the Durants so well put it, "When he returned from England he brought Newton and Locke in his baggage; he spent part of his next twenty years introducing them to France."[5]

The fourteenth letter of his *Letters concerning the English Nation* was devoted to Newton and his findings, and to his ardent recommendation to the French to embrace Newton. Subsequently, he wrote a full-length exposition of Newton's work, a 440-page book entitled *Eléments de la philosophie de Newton*,[6] published in 1741, two years before Condorcet's birth. It was an exposition suitable as a lay person's introduction to a difficult subject, designed also to persuade acceptance of Newton's work as a disclosure of scientific truth.

The extent of Newton's influence can be measured by the fact that before the French Revolution began in 1789, eighteen editions of the *Principia* were issued. In addition an avalanche of popular accounts had been published, of which forty were in English and seventeen in French.[7] Newton and his work were also included in that great and influential compendium of knowledge and enlightened ideas—the *Encyclopédie*.

When Newton died in 1727, at the age of eighty-five, he was so esteemed, so much a national hero, that at the conclusion of his funeral, witnessed by Voltaire, he was accorded in death his last, full honor—acceptance in Westminster Abbey.

Locke

There is an aphorism attributed to the philosophes that suggests the importance they attached to knowing the work of both Newton and Locke. It seems to have been designed as a prescription for a clear and simple way of understanding science and human affairs. Concerning science, it prescribes, "Follow Newton and all is clear," and, with reference to human affairs, "Begin with Locke and all follows."[8]

John Locke was the son of a country lawyer who also served for a while as a clerk to the justices of the peace in Somerset. The son, destined to be distinguished and famous, arrived on the scene in Wrington, Somerset, in 1632, ten years before Newton's birth.

While Newton was educated at Cambridge, Locke was a product of Christ Church, Oxford. Thus both great institutions can point to seventeenth-century intellectual luminaries as members of their illustrious alumni. Unlike Newton, who seems to have known from the beginning that his career was to be in mathematics and science, Locke appears to have long been uncertain concerning his niche in life. He received his B.A. in 1656 and remained in residence at the university to acquire a master's degree and to serve as a lecturer in Greek rhetoric and philosophy.

His father's death in 1661, when Locke was twenty-nine, left him with a small inheritance. He thereupon chose to study medicine, but never became a practicing physician. About a year after his father's death, in one of those fortuitous happenings that sometimes shape a career, he met Anthony Ashley Cooper, the Earl of Shaftesbury, at Oxford.

Shaftesbury was actively engaged in the political life of England during the reign of Charles II from 1660 to 1685. Winston Churchill, who was, to say the least, a political analyst of considerable talent, described Shaftesbury in his *History of the English Speaking Peoples* as "the second greatest parliamentary tactician of the century."[9] During the course of his career, Shaftesbury was Chancellor of the Exchequer and Lord Chancellor. However, the times were troubled and turbulent and there were occasions when he was out of favor and, at the end of his life, so much out of favor, that in 1682 he fled to Holland for safety, where he died in 1683.

Despite the disparities in their social standing and talents, their personalities were congenial, and Locke and Shaftesbury hit it off nicely. Locke became Shaftesbury's friend, personal physician, and respected adviser. As a consequence Locke's fortunes ebbed and flowed with Shaftesbury's. When Shaftesbury was in favor, Locke was favored in a variety of capacities that kept him involved in the political life of the time and very much a man of the world in practical affairs. When Shaftesbury was in disfavor, Locke, too, was affected. As a result he spent four years in France between 1675 and 1679, and when Shaftesbury fled to Holland, Locke followed suit and remained in Holland from 1683 to 1689.

Locke began the work for which he is noted in England while serving as a practical man of affairs. During his years abroad as a man of the world, he found time to socialize and acquire a wide circle of distinguished friends. Nevertheless, when he was forced to live outside of England as a result of his association with Shaftesbury and was consequently disengaged from active participation in the practical affairs of English political life, he used the opportunity and the time to devote himself seriously to his real mission in life—pursuing the life of a philosopher engaged in the study of human nature and of government and commiting his reflections to paper.

In 1689 and 1690, shortly after his return to England, the two great works with which his name has since been associated were published: his *Essay Concerning Human Understanding* and the *Two Treatises of Government*.

The subject of the *Essay* is learning—how we learn. It presented a persuasive case against the concept that we are born with innate ideas, a point of view that appealed to political and religious absolutists. Interested in the preservation of their positions of authority, it was convenient for them to support the notion that the desire to submit to authority is present in men's minds from birth. Locke argued in the *Essay* that the human mind at birth is a "tabula rasa," a blank slate, and that our ideas are derived from experience. In his words:

> Let us suppose then the mind to be, as we say, white paper, void of all characters, without any ideas:—How comes it to be furnished? Whence comes it by that vast store which the busy and boundless fancy of man has painted on it with an almost endless variety? Whence has it all the materials of reason and knowledge? To this I answer, in one word, from Experience.[10]

In Locke's analysis, as expressed in the *Essay*, experience generates our ideas both through the sensations that we receive from external sources and through the internal operations of our minds upon those sensations. To refer again to Locke's words:

> Our observations employed either about external sensible objects, or about the internal operations of our minds perceived and reflected on by ourselves, is that which supplies our understandings with all the materials of thinking. These two are the fountains of knowledge from whence all the ideas we have, can naturally have, do spring.[11]

Accordingly Locke can be classified as both an empiricist and a rationalist since he attributed the source of our ideas to experience and to reason or, as is sometimes said, to sensation and to reflection.

The *Essay Concerning Human Understanding* is also the foundation for the *Two Treatises on Government*. The two works are complementary. In view of the closeness of their dates of publication it is difficult to escape the conclusion that the themes of the two works were intimately related in Locke's mind. They form a consistent pattern of thought in which the analysis of the *Essay* leads inevitably to the thesis of the *Two Treatises*. The first treatise carries forward the argument against innate ideas, as they relate to the source of authority in government, to the logical conclusion that no one is invested with the divine right to be a ruler.

Sir Richard Filmer, in a book entitled *Patriarcha*, had predicated his argument that there is a divine right to rule on the contention that it is a right derived from Adam, who, he claimed, had been divinely appointed as monarch of the world. Locke used Filmer's argument as a point of departure for the presentation of his theory of the source of power in government, pointing out, on the way, that even if Filmer's assumption were correct that Adam had been divinely so appointed, none of the current monarchs, including the king of England, could trace the legitimacy of their authority to Adam.

Denying the validity of the assumption of the divine right to rule through inheritance from Adam, the second treatise presents an entirely different theory about the source of authority to govern. Locke argues that human beings initially lived in a state of nature, in which each enjoyed "a state of perfect freedom to order their actions and dispose of their possessions and persons as they think fit, within the bounds of the Law of Nature, without asking leave, or depending upon the will of any other man."[12] Subsequently, according to Locke, people entered into a social contract to organize a political society because an organized society is a better way to protect the rights of life, liberty, and property than one that is unorganized.

Because, in this analysis, the social contract is made by consenting members of the community, sovereignty rests not with a ruler, monarch, or otherwise, but with the people who give their consent. Therefore, for the same reason, executives and legislators serve as agents of the sovereign people. Accordingly, since the objective of men in making and adhering to the social contract is the protection of their lives, their freedom, and their property, any assumption of dominance and exercise of authority by one of them over others constitutes, in effect, an act of war against the others, giving them the right to rebel.[13]

As in the case of Newton's *Principia*, the *Essay* and the *Two Treatises* were immediately recognized and acclaimed as important contributions to thought and Locke became both celebrated and revered as the philosopher of freedom. Newton was among the many who visited him to pay respects. As one writer has said, "England at this time was firmly in the grip of the philosophy of the son of a country lawyer. Seldom can a philosopher have had greater power than that enjoyed by John Locke."[14]

Locke's influence on eighteenth-century French thought was equally significant. As previously noted, when Voltaire, the most influential man in France, returned from exile "he brought Newton and Locke in his baggage"[15] and, for many years thereafter, he was a very effective apostle of Locke as well as of Newton. In the thirteenth letter of his *Letters concerning the English Nation*, Voltaire "found in" Locke "not only a science of the mind instead of a mythology of the soul but an implicit philosophy that, by tracing all knowledge to sensation, turned European thought from divine revelation to human experience as the exclusive source and basis of truth."[16]

Equally telling in an appraisal of Locke's influence on French thought in the eighteenth century is the fact that d'Alembert in his celebrated introduction to the *Encyclopédie*, known as the *Discours Préliminaire*, unreservedly adopted Locke's idea about the process of learning, saying that "it is to sensations that we owe all our ideas."[17] There is justification, therefore, for the conclusion expressed by the Durants in their fine study of the Age of Voltaire, that "next to Bacon, the strongest influence in the *Encyclopédie* was that of Locke."[18] Locke's thought attained international influence[19] through the *Encyclopedie*, a work that, in the words of the Roman Catholic critic Brunetière, was "the great affair of its time, the goal to which everything preceding it was tending, the origin of everything that followed it, and consequently the true center for any history of ideas in the eighteenth century."[20]

Notes

1. Cardinal Richelieu also died in 1642.

2. Leibniz is generally considered to be a simultaneous inventor of calculus.

3. William H. Harris and Judith S. Levey, eds., *The New Columbia Encyclopedia*, 4th ed. (New York: Columbia University Press, 1975), p. 1929.

4. *Principia*, Book III.

5. Will and Ariel Durant, *The Age of Voltaire*, vol. 9 of *The Story of Civilization* (New York: Simon and Schuster, 1965), p. 248.

6. Without Voltaire's permission, an edition was printed in Amsterdam in 1738.

7. See John H. Randall, Jr., *Making of the Modern Mind: A Survey of the Intellectual Background of the Present Age*, rev. ed. (New York: Columbia University Press, 1976), p. 260. Of the remaining seventy-three accounts of Newton's work, three were published in German, eleven in Latin, one in Portuguese, and one in Italian (ibid., p. 260).

8. John A. Garraty and Peter Gay, eds., *The Columbia History*

of the World (New York: Columbia University Press, 1990), p. 701.

9. Winston S. Churchill, *History of the English Speaking Peoples* (New York: Dodd, Mead & Company, 1956), vol. 2, p. 357.

10. *Essay Concerning Human Understanding* 2.1.2.

11. Ibid.

12. *Two Treatises on Government* 2.2.4.

13. Locke returned to England at the time of the accession of William of Orange and Mary to the throne in 1689, an event known as the "Glorious Revolution." It has been said that the revolution was "consecrated by the superb rationale of John Locke's second treatise on government" (*The Columbia History of the World*, p. 582).

14. James Burke, *The Day the Universe Changed* (Boston: Little, Brown and Company, 1987), p. 175.

15. W. and A. Durant, *The Age of Voltaire*, p. 248.

16. Ibid., p. 369.

17. Ibid., p. 636.

18. Ibid.

19. The influence of Newton and Locke on American thought in the eighteenth century is notable in the Declaration of Independence. The opening paragraph is reminiscent of Newton in its reference to the "Laws of Nature and Nature's God," incorporating the concept of a universe governed by the universally applicable laws of nature. The second paragraph adopts Locke's contract theory that governments are instituted among men to secure "certain unalienable rights" including "Life, Liberty and the Pursuit of Happiness" and the right to revolt "whenever any form of government becomes destructive of these rights."

20. W. and A. Durant, *The Age of Voltaire*, p. 633. The Durants cite as authority for the above quote, "Brunetière, *Evolution des genres dans l'histoire de la literature* (Paris, 1890), 210." See also Arthur M. Wilson, *Diderot* (Oxford: Oxford University Press, 1972), p. 169.

6

Rousseau

No estimate of eighteenth-century French thought would be complete without consideration of the influence of Jean-Jacques Rousseau. He was born in Geneva in 1712, three years before the death of Louis XIV, and died in 1778, the year of the death of Voltaire. By then, he was Voltaire's equal in fame. He was a close friend of Diderot and a contributor to the *Encyclopédie*, and for a time he was considered one of the philosophes. But always the emotional romantic, he was the very antithesis of such men as Newton and Locke in the essential cast of his mind, and so he had little in common with the new interest in science and reason shared by the other philosophes.

In 1750, when he was thirty-eight (and Condorcet was seven), he first achieved the notice that led to fame. The Academy of Dijon had announced a contest in 1749 for the best essay on the subject of "whether the sciences and arts had contributed to the corruption or the improvement of human conduct."[1] Rousseau's essay, entitled *Discours sur les sciences et les arts* (Discourse on the sciences and arts) was the winner and an almost instant popular success.

The *Discours* foretold the direction of Rousseau's thinking. He portrayed an original scene of idyllic simplicity and innocence in an imagined golden age when humans lived in a state of natural goodness, a time when "men were innocent and virtuous."[2] The *Discours* reflected his conviction that the sciences and arts had been a corrupting influence, despoiling the natural goodness of the human being and leading mankind downward on a path of decadence and corruption. After detailing the maladies of character and conduct afflicting civilized people, Rousseau made this condemnatory peroration: "Let the arts and sciences claim the share they have had in this salutary work!"[3] Many years later he wrote a letter to Malesherbes describing the way he felt at the moment when he learned about the contest. He said he was moved to demonstrate that "man is by nature good and that only our institutions have made him bad."[4]

At another point the *Discours* relates this parable about the utility of books:

> It is related that the Caliph Omar being asked what should be done with the library of Alexandria answered . . . , "If the books in the library contain anything contrary to the Alcoran, they are evil and ought to be burned; if they contain only what the Alcoran teaches, they are superfluous." This reasoning has been cited by our men of letters as the height of absurdity; but if Gregory the Great had been in the place of Omar, and the Gospel in the place of the Alcoran, the library would still have been burned, and it would have been perhaps the finest action of his life.[5]

From Rousseau's point of view the invention of printing was an unfortunate event. It was his opinion that "sovereigns will hereafter take as much pains to banish this dreadful art from their dominions, as they ever took to encourage it."[6]

Burning books and banishing printing was not the line of thought in which the philosophes believed or which they advocated. It was inevitable that Rousseau and the philosophes would part company. Eight years later that break occurred. Rousseau chose to disassociate himself from the philosophes at a time when the *Encyclopédie* was threatened with suppression. In October 1758, he published an essay of 135 pages in the form of a letter addressed to d'Alembert, entitled *Lettre à M. d'Alembert sur les spectacles* (Letter to Mr. d'Alembert about shows). As the Durants have said, "It was . . . a declaration of war against the Age of Reason." It was also the vehicle that Rousseau used to terminate his friendship with Diderot.

This severance of relationships was occasioned by the fact that d'Alembert had written an article for the *Encyclopedie* on the subject of Geneva in which he had urged the Genevan authorities to permit the presentation of plays. The idea of introducing into the pristine life of Geneva what Rousseau conceived to be the corrupting influence of the theater was sufficient to arouse the writing of his denunciation and the termination of his relationship to the philosophes.

In 1756 Rousseau began the writing of a novel, published in Holland in 1761, entitled *Julie or Nouvelle Héloise, Lettres de deux amants recueillies et publiées par J.-J. Rousseau* (Julia or the new Héloise, letters of two lovers gathered and published by J.-J. Rousseau). The *New Héloise* illustrates, in the form of a love story, Rousseau's conviction about the superiority of feelings over intellect. Dripping with emotion and sentimentality, it extols feeling as a better guide than reason in the difficult business of living. The novel is presented in the form of an exchange of letters supposedly written by Julie, the daughter of

Baron d'Étrange, and Saint Preux, a handsome young man who is engaged to be Julie's tutor when she is seventeen.

It is doubtful that Julie's intellectual development could have been enhanced by Saint Preux's tutelage since the two are quickly involved in the entrancing throes of passionate love. A paragraph from a Saint Preux letter indicates the novel's effusive expressions of feeling:

> Celestial Powers. . . . Inspire me with a soul that can bear felicity! Divine love! spirit of my existence, oh support me, for I am ready to sink down under the weight of ecstacy! Oh, how shall I withstand the rapid torrent of bliss which overflows my heart?—and how dispel the apprehension of a timorously loving girl?

While this flowery language would probably be considered excessive and insincere by most twentieth-century readers, it nevertheless struck a responsive note in the psyche of not only French readers of the eighteenth century, but those of England and Germany as well. It was an enormous success.

Three years after Rousseau won the prize awarded by the Dijon Academy for his *Discourse on the Arts and Sciences,* he was inspired to think and write once more, this time about the subject of equality as a result of the announcement of another prize competition, instituted again by the Dijon Academy. In November 1753, the question at issue was this: "What is the origin of inequality among men, and is it authorized by natural law?" Rousseau did not win the competition on this occasion, but his response to the Dijon Academy, published by him in 1755, again excited wide public attention.

That response, entitled *Discours sur l'origine et les fondements de l'inégalité parmi les hommes* (Discourse on the origin and the foundations of inequality among men), recognized that there are biological differences that distinguish men. "I conceive," he said, "two kinds of inequality among the human species; one which I call natural or physical because it is established by nature . . . and another, which may be called moral or political inequality, because it depends on a kind of convention, and is established, or at least authorized by the consent of man."[7] In his analysis, moral or political inequality was one of the evils of civilization, attributable to the acquisition of property. As he said, "The first man who, having enclosed a piece of ground, bethought himself of saying 'This is mine,' and found people simple enough to believe him, was the real founder of civil society."[8]

According to Rousseau, the acquisition of property led to inequality and to conflict among men, the creation of the rich and the poor, the powerful and the weak and, inevitably, to a constant state of strife and war. Ultimately this condition, the insecurity that it engendered, and the need of the rich and powerful to protect their possessions and safety led to "the profoundest plan that ever entered the mind of man"—the legalization of title, to property by the creation of the institution of the state[9]:

> Let us join to guard the weak from oppression, to restrain the ambitious, and to secure to every man the possession of what belongs to him. . . . Let us, in a word, instead of turning our forces on ourselves, collect them in a supreme power and maintain eternal harmony among us.[10]

Beguiled and ensnared by this intriguing idea, Rousseau says,

> All ran headlong to their chains, in hopes of securing their liberty; for they had just wit enough to perceive the advan-

tages of political institutions, without experience enough to enable them to forsee their dangers.[11]

The consequence was that through the establishment of political institutions and laws that they designed, the rich and the powerful perpetuated their status at the expense of the poor and the weak and, in Rousseau's melancholy opinion,

> irretrievably destroyed natural liberty, eternally fixed the laws of property and inequality, converted clever usurpation into unalterable right, and, for the advantage of a few ambitious individuals, subjected all mankind to perpetual labour, slavery and wretchedness.[12]

The inequality of men and their lack of freedom must have been a constant preoccupation of Rousseau, for he returned to that problem again in the most important work of his career, *Du Contrat social* (The social contract), discreetly published, undoubtedly with the censor in mind, in the safe haven of Holland, in the year 1762.[13] That exercise of discretion was assuredly a wise one, for the first chapter begins with the incendiary outcry: "Man is born free; and everywhere he is in chains."

The work is subtitled *Principes du droit politique* (Principles of political right), indicating that it is a philosophical discussion of political rights as they should be, rather than a description of existing governments. As he stated in his introduction, he is taking "men—as they are" and "laws as they might be."[14]

In this analysis of principles, Rousseau endeavored to provide a prescription for remedying both the inequality of men and their lack of freedom in a social order far removed from the benign "state of nature." As he said, in explaining his motivation for writing *The Social Contract*, "To renounce liberty is to renounce being a man. . . . Such a renunciation is incompatible with man's nature; to remove all liberty from his will is to remove all morality from his acts."[15] His quest, therefore, as he stated it, was "to find a form of association which will defend and protect, with the whole common force, the persons and goods of each associate, and in which each, while uniting himself with all, may still obey himself alone, and remain as free as before."[16] His prescription is embraced in the concepts of the "social contract," the "general will," and "sovereignty."

In his version of the contract theory of government, Rousseau adopted as his thesis the idea of a social contract in which a whole society agrees to be governed by its "general will." "Each of us," he said, "puts his person, and all his powers in common under the supreme direction of the general will, and in our corporate capacity, we receive each member as an indivisible part of the whole."[17] The "general will" in Rousseau's analysis is the key to the maintenance of the happy state in which men are free and equal.

The premise of the general will is the characteristic that distinguishes Rousseau's theory of the social contract from prior versions of the theory. Previous constructions of the theory had treated the social contract as a political agreement between people who agreed to be governed and a single person or a small group of persons who agreed to be their governors. They governed and the people allowed themselves to be governed. In the free society envisioned by Rousseau, governed by the "general will," the people are sovereign and "the deputies of the people . . . are not and cannot be its representatives; they are merely its stewards."[18]

In much of the analysis of *The Social Contract* there is an affinity of ideas and goals between Rousseau and the philosophes. In the stress on the importance of equality and liberty, the repudiation, expressed or implied, of the divine right of kings, and the assertion of the sovereignty of the people they see eye to eye. But there the affinity ends. On the subject of liberty they are divided by a wide chasm of differences.

Rousseau was led by the logic of his ideology concerning the "general will" to adopt a concept of freedom that is inhospitable to the individual's "unalienable right" to liberty. On the rigid premise, based on the theory of the "general will," that "obedience to a law which we prescribe for ourselves is liberty,"[19] Rousseau concluded that the individual "shall be obliged to observe the general will" and that "this means nothing less than that he will be forced to be free."[20]

In another version of the same thought in which the logic of ideology challenges the logic of common sense, he says:

> When in the General Assembly a law is proposed, what the people [are] asked is not exactly whether [they] approve . . . or reject . . . the proposal, but whether it is in conformity with the general will, which is their will. Each man in giving his vote, states his opinion whether it is in conformity with the general will, which is their will. Each man in giving his vote, states his opinion upon that point; and the general will is found by counting votes. When therefore the opinion that is contrary to my own prevails, this proves neither more nor less than that I was mistaken, and that what I thought to be the general will was not so. If my particular opinion had carried the day, I should have achieved the opposite of what was my will, and it is in that case that I should not have been free.[21]

This is a program for conformity, a procrustean rule for the suppression of dissent. It authorizes a majority to be intolerant, censorial, and even despotic toward a minority.

Such a program was inconsistent with the outlook of the

philosophes, who were steadfast in their commitment to freedom, pragmatic in their thinking, and dedicated to the life of reason and to the overriding idea of the achievement of liberty for people, uninhibited by an inflexible theory of government. The *Encyclopédie's* article on government put the matter simply and crisply and without qualification: "The people's greatest good is its liberty. . . . Without liberty happiness is banished from states."[22]

But above all the philosophy of *The Social Contract* projected a spirit of intolerance toward dissent, religious as well as political, notably at odds with the point of view of the philosophes and strikingly so in the matter of religious belief. At the end of the final version of *The Social Contract,* Rousseau proposed the introduction into the life of the state of a civil religion to which every citizen would be required to adhere. Denial of the dogmas of this religion was to be impermissible. Then came this extraordinary sentence: "If anyone, after publicly recognizing these dogmas, behaves as if he does not believe them, let him be punished by death."[23]

This was, to say the least, a different idea about religion than the one that appealed to the philosophes. They, unlike Rousseau, were subscribers to the happy state of diversity in religious belief as the assurance of tolerance for the liberty of all. As Voltaire said, in religion as in politics, "toleration is a necessity." The contrast between Rousseau and Voltaire on this subject is underscored in a letter written by Voltaire to Mme. du Deffand. Noting that the laws of England had restored the rights from which every man had been "despoiled" by monarchy, he enumerated among the restored rights not only freedom of person, property, and press but, in addition, the right "to profess whatever religion he prefers."[24]

Despite the wide popularity of Rousseau's ideas, especially his exposition of the superiority of feeling over reason, it is devotion to the life of reason that is the trademark of the eighteenth century. Voltaire, rather than Rousseau, best expresses the spirit of the Age of Enlightenment.[25] It is safe to say, without deprecating the importance of feeling and sentiment in the conduct of human relations, that reason played the major role in the eighteenth century in the liberation of the human mind from the repressive authority exercised by both church and state over the very human desire for independence in thinking and for self-expression. After two centuries of time for considered review and reflection, the eighteenth century continues to be known, appropriately, as the Age of Enlightenment and, synonymously, as the Age of Reason,[26] precisely because it was an age notably devoted to the life of reason.

The liberation of mind resulting from the ascendancy of reason helped to provide the climate and the rationale in our country for the establishment of the democratic way of life, expressed in the Declaration of Independence, the Constitution, and the Bill of Rights, and for the release here and abroad of that remarkable burst of scientific inquiry and knowledge—freed from the restraints imposed by church and state—that occurred in the nineteenth and twentieth centuries. Despite Rousseau's jaundiced view of books, printing, and learning, the business of publication continues to flourish, and both the sciences and the arts have grown since his time, especially the sciences, which have produced our current "information explosion."

Rousseau's philosophy also diverged sharply from the philosophes' commitment to the spirit of progress, a subject of intense interest to Condorcet. The eighteenth century's enormous optimism and confidence in the future was stimulated, in part, by the contributions of Newton and Locke to knowledge. Their work was a convincing display of the power of reason. If it could unravel the profound mystery of the laws governing the universe and that other deep "puzzlement"—the operation of the human mind—it was reasonable to believe that in the pursuit of progress its possibilities were limitless.

By contrast, Rousseau's pessimistic point of view held that the sciences, the arts, books, and printing were corrupting human nature and leading men and women downward and away from a time of goodness, idyllic simplicity, and happiness.

Condorcet, obviously, did not share this view. His *Sketch* conveyed to posterity his profound attachment to the idea of progress and his confidence in a future of infinite promise.

Notes

1. The theme of the essay contest has been translated in a variety of ways: "Has the progress of the sciences and arts contributed to the corruption or to the improvement of human conduct?"—William H. Harris and Judith S. Levey, eds. *The New Columbia Encyclopedia,* 4th ed. (New York: Columbia University Press, 1975), p. 2365; "Whether the restoration of the arts and sciences has contributed to the purification of manners"—Paul Edwards, ed., *Encyclopedia of Philosophy* (New York: Free Press, 1973), vol. 7, p. 219; "Has the restoration of the sciences and the arts contributed to corrupt or to purify morals?"—W. and A. Durant, *Rousseau and Revolution,* vol. 10 of *The Story of Civilization* (New York: Simon and Schuster, 1967), p. 19.

2. See Rousseau, *The Social Contract and Discourses,* rev. ed., trans. G. D. H. Cole (Rutland, Vt.: C. E. Tuttle, 1991, Everyman's Classic Library), p. 164, hereafter referred to as Rousseau, Everyman edition.

3. Ibid., p. 150. On the same page Rousseau says, "Our minds have been corrupted as the arts and sciences have improved."

4. The letter is dated January 12, 1762. See W. and A. Durant, *The Age of Voltaire,* vol. 9 of *The Story of Civilization* (New York: Simon and Schuster, 1965), p. 19.

5. Rousseau, Everyman edition, p. 171. The references to Omar and to Gregory the Great probably relate to Umar, the second caliph (c. 634–644) and to Saint Gregory the Great, who was pope from 590 to 604. Alcoran is better known as the Koran.

6. Rousseau, Everyman edition, p. 171. It was, of course, the printed word that gave Rousseau his own notable success, a fact that Voltaire tactfully but pointedly stressed in a letter to Rousseau, phrased in the carefully chosen words of a skilled diplomat: "Literature nourishes the soul, corrects it, consoles it; it makes your glory at the same time that you write against it." (From a letter of Voltaire to Rousseau acknowledging the receipt from Rousseau of a copy of his *Discours sur l'origine et les fondements de l'inegalité parmi les hommes.*)

7. Rousseau, Everyman edition, p. 196.

8. Ibid., p. 234.

9. Ibid., p. 250.

10. Ibid., p. 251.

11. Ibid.

12. Ibid., pp. 251–52.

13. *Emile*, Rousseau's famous work on the subject of education, was also published in 1762.

14. Rousseau, Everyman edition, p. 3. Rousseau's philosophical approach to "laws as they might be" contrasts with Montesquieu's factual study of the operations of the institutions of states as they actually were.

15. In Book I, chapter 6, page 13 of the *Social Contract* (Everyman edition), Rousseau again refers to the "state of nature," a hypothetical original condition of mankind, presumed to have been marked by simplicity, innocence, and virtue. It is an assumption that underlies the two *Discourses* as well as the *Social Contract*. Sir Henry Sumner Maine (1822–1888),who pioneered the historical and comparative study of institutions, including law, made these critical observations about Rousseau and the state of nature:

Now, in all the speculations of Rousseau, the central figure, whether arrayed in an English dress as the signatory of a social compact, or simply stripped of all historical qualities, is uniformly man, in a supposed state of nature. It is not worth our while to analyze with any particularity that philosophy of politics, art, education, ethics, and social relations which was constructed on the basis of a state of nature. It still presents singular fascination for the looser thinkers of every country and is no doubt the parent . . . of almost all the prepossessions which impede the Historical method of inquiry. (*Ancient Law* [Oxford: Oxford University Press, The World Classics], pp. 72 and 73.)

16. Rousseau, Everyman edition, Book I, ch. 5, pp. 13–14.

17. Ibid., Book I, ch. 6, p. 15. The Social Contract theory is not original with Rousseau. Among many instances it appears in Locke's *Treatises on Civil Government*, previously discussed.

18. Ibid., Bk. III, ch. 13, p. 94.

19. Ibid., Bk. I, ch. 8, p. 19: "The mere impulse of appetite is slavery, while obedience to a law which we prescribe to ourselves is liberty."

20. Ibid., Bk. I, ch. 8, p. 18.

21. Ibid.

22. See W. and A. Durant, *The Age of Voltaire*, p. 641.

23. Rousseau, Everyman edition, Bk. IV, ch. 8, p. 139.

24. See W. and A. Durant, *The Age of Voltaire*, p. 247.

25. In *Rousseau and Revolution* the Durants expressed the opinion that "after 1760 the eighteenth century belonged to Rousseau" (p. 170).

26. See, for example, references to the eighteenth century as the Age of Enlightenment and, synonymously, the Age of Reason in John A Garraty and Peter Gay, eds., *Columbia History of the World* (New York: Columbia University Press, 1990), p. 696; Pierre Coubert, *Louis XIV and the Twenty Million Frenchmen* (New York: Vintage Books, 1972), p. 14; and W. and A. Durant, *Rousseau and Revolution*, p. 20.

7

Montesquieu

Charles-Louis de Secondat, Baron de la Brède et de Montesquieu, is better known to us today simply as Montesquieu. Born in 1689 near Bordeaux, during the reign of Louis XIV, he lived the easy life of a landed aristocrat, inheriting a barony from an uncle and, with it, membership in, and later the presidency of, the Bordeaux parliament. He was also a member of the *noblesse de robe* and the *noblesse d'épée*. He died in 1755, at the age of sixty-five, during the reign of Louis XV.

This great writer and thinker made his contribution to the Enlightenment through two influential works—the *Persian Letters* and the *Spirit of Laws*. The first, published anonymously in Holland in 1721, was an immediate success, so popular that ten editions were printed in one year. It has been said that the *Persian Letters* and Voltaire's subsequent *Letters on the English* (1734) had the effect of inaugurating the Age of Enlightenment.[1]

The *Persian Letters* purport to be a translation by Montesquieu of letters written to family and friends in Persia by two Persian visitors to France, named Usbek and Rica. This format provided the vehicle for satiric, ironic, and highly critical comments about French life in the guise of the allegedly naive reactions of strangers in France, who, naturally enough, are curious, at times fascinated, and sometimes supposedly astonished by what they see, hear, and learn. Under this protective cloak, Montesquieu even engaged in derogatory criticism of the monarchy and the person of the king.

Letter 85, for example, written by Usbek to one Mirza at Ispahan is caustic in its criticism of the intolerance and stupidity of the Grand Monarch's revocation of the Edict of Nantes. That edict, it will be recalled, granted religious freedom to the Huguenots. Its revocation by Louis XIV and the consequent relegation of French Protestants to the status of outlaws led about 200,000 of them to flee from France with subsequent serious damage to the French economy. In this instance Uzbek's letter takes the form of a parable transparently intended to castigate the intolerance and the blunder of Louis XIV.

Once, as you know, Mirza, some of Shah Suleiman's ministers made a plan to force all the Armenians in Persia either to leave the kingdom or to become Muslims, in the belief that our empire would be contaminated as long as infidels remained within it.

It would have put an end to the greatness of Persia if blind religious piety had had its way on this occasion.

Nobody knows why it came to nothing. Neither those who made the proposal, nor those who rejected it, foresaw the consequences; it was chance that took over the functions of reason and good government, and saved the empire from a danger greater than if it had been defeated in battle and suffered the loss of two towns.

To have proscribed the Armenians would have meant wiping out in a single day all the business men and almost all the skilled workers in the kingdom.

The letter concludes with these observations:

> For after all, even if there were no inhumanity in doing violence
> to other people's consciences, even if it produced none of the
> bad effects which flow from it in thousands, one would have
> to be out of one's mind to think of it.[2]

Religious leaders and religious programs and practices did
not escape the searching scrutiny and, at times, the scorn of the
Letters. Letter 29, attributed by Montesquieu to Rica, opens with
this critical statement:

> The Pope is the chief of the Christians; he is an ancient idol,
> worshipped now from habit. . . . He claims to be the successor
> of one of the earliest Christians, Saint Peter, and it is certainly
> a rich successor, for his treasure is immense and he has a great
> country under his control.

Of the Bishops, Rica reports:

> When they are on their own, virtually their only function is
> to dispense people from obedience to the Christian law. For
> you must know that this religion is burdened with an infinity
> of very difficult observances; and so, considering that it is less
> easy to fulfil these duties than to have bishops who give dis-
> pensations, the latter course has been adopted as a matter of
> public policy.

Then Montesquieu, through his mouthpiece, makes these dis-
paraging observations on the subject of heretics:

> Those who bring out some new propositions are immediately
> declared heretics. Each heresy has its name, which for those

who are committed to it serves as a password. But nobody
is a heretic against his will. All he has to do is to split the
difference of opinion into two halves, and provide a distinction
for those who accuse him of heresy, and whatever the distinction
may be, intelligible or not, it makes a man as white as snow,
and he can have himself declared orthodox.

What I say applies to France and Germany; for I have heard
that in Spain and Portugal there are certain dervishes who
cannot see a joke, and who burn a man as they would straw. . . .

Other judges presume that the accused is innocent; these
always presume him guilty. When in doubt, they opt for severity
on principle, apparently because they believe that men are wicked.

When passing sentence they pay their respects in a little
speech . . . and say that they are lenient and detest bloodshed,
and that they are in despair at having condemned them to death.
But to console themselves they confiscate for their own benefit
everything that the poor wretches possess.[3]

Theologians and their doctrinal disputes are also targets of
Montesquieu's wit:

There is an infinite number of theologians, mostly dervishes,
and they raise thousands of new questions about religion among
themselves. They are left to argue for a long time, and the war
goes on until a decision arrives to end it.

So that I can assure you that no kingdom ever had as many
civil wars as the kingdom of Christ.[4]

Resorting to the experience provided by history, Montesquieu
turns from the critical to the positive and extols freedom as the
way of reason. Thus, in Letter 131, ostensibly written to Rica
by a Persian correspondent who appears to be a student of history,
reflecting on "the glory that was Greece,"[5] he observes:

Love of freedom and hatred of kings preserved Greek independence for a long time and extended republican government
to distant parts [such as Asia Minor, Italy, and Spain]. These
Greek settlements brought with them a spirit of freedom which
they had acquired in their own delightful country. All this was
in Europe; as for Asia and Africa, they have always been crushed
under despotism, if you except the few towns of Asia Minor
which we have mentioned, and the City of Carthage in Africa.[6]

Then in Letter 136, following the theme of Letter 131, Montesquieu equates freedom with "reason, humanity, and nature."
Referring to the decline of the "mighty Roman Empire," as a result
of the invasions of the "barbarian peoples" from the north, he
concludes:

These people were not truly barbarous, since they were free,
but they have become so now that most of them have submitted
to dictatorship, and lost the sweetness of freedom, which is
in such close concord with reason, humanity and nature.[7]

In 1727, six years after the Persian Letters were published,
Montesquieu began to work on the project that occupied his
thoughts for the next twenty years and resulted in the publication
in 1748 of his masterpiece—*D'Esprit des lois* (The spirit of laws).
During this time, he traveled to England, for a sojourn of eighteen
months, and like Voltaire, he was impressed with English government and the freedom of the English. After returning in 1731,
he retired to his estate at La Bréde and devoted the rest of his
life to study and writing. That, incidentally, is the reason that
I think of him as a philosopher rather than a philosophe, one
of whose hallmarks was sustained active participation in life
outside the ivory tower.

Bearing a somewhat elaborate title, namely, *On the Spirit of Laws or the Relationships which Laws Must Have to the Constitution of Each Government, to Mores, Climate, Religion, Commerce, etc.,* the *Spirit of Laws* combined a historical and sociological approach to the philosophy of government. In accordance with the precaution still needed in France in 1748, the book was published in Geneva in two unsigned volumes. Also in accordance with the spirit of the time, it was promptly condemned by the French clergy, placed on the Index, and, by order of the government, its distribution in France was forbidden. In 1750, Malesherbe, the very model of a gentle censor, revoked the prohibition.

The *Spirit of Laws* was recognized almost immediately as an outstanding contribution to the philosophy of government. Its influence, evidenced by twenty-two editions published in two years and its translation into many European languages, extended far beyond the borders of France even to the distant colonies across the sea that later became the United States.[8]

Emile Durkheim (1858–1917), the eminent French sociologist and one of the founders of modern sociology, said that Montesquieu's *Spirit of Laws* gave modern sociology both its method and field of study. However, in the context of his influence on the Enlightenment and on Condorcet, it is Montesquieu the humanitarian and rationalist, and the opponent of slavery, aggressive wars, cruel punishment, despotism, and religious intolerance, who engages our attention.[9]

His most enduring contribution to the theory of government is his persuasive argument, in the interest of liberty, for checks and balances by means of the separation of powers—an idea that is imbedded in our Constitution by its provisions for the division of authority between the President, the Congress, and the Supreme Court.[10] The following paragraphs illustrate the vital importance that Montesquieu attached to the concept that the protection of liberty is the central function of government and that the means for its accomplishment is the separation of powers:

> When the legislative and executive powers are united in the same person, or in the same body of magistrates, there can be no liberty, because apprehension may arise, lest the same monarch or senate should enact tyrannical laws, to execute them in a tyrannical manner.
>
> Again, there is no liberty, if the judiciary power be not separated from the legislative and executive. Were it joined with the legislative the life and liberty of the subject would be exposed to arbitrary control; for the judge would then be the legislator. Were it joined to the executive power, the judge might behave with violence and oppression.[11]

Notes

1. In *The Age of Voltaire,* vol. 9 of *The Story of Civilization* (New York: Simon & Schuster, 1965), p. 344, Will and Ariel Durant say that "these two books announced the Enlightenment."

2. Montesquieu, *Persian Letters,* trans. C. J. Betts (New York: Penguin Classics, 1973), pp. 164–66.

3. Ibid., pp. 81–82.

4. Ibid.

5. P. B. Shelley, *Adonais.*

6. Montesquieu, *Persian Letters,* pp. 233–34.

7. Ibid., p. 241.

8. In the *Origins of the French Revolution* (Oxford: Oxford University Press, Student Edition, 1988), p. 85, William Doyle says, "Anyone who reads the remonstrances of the parlements in the later eighteenth century will find them steeped (conspicuously or otherwise) in the ideas

of Montesquieu."

9. "The idea of despotism as the eighteenth century understood it had first emerged among critics of Louis XIV's arbitrary, unrestrained method of government. But it was given its classic definition in 1748 by Montesquieu in his *Esprit des Lois*" (ibid., p. 87).

10. "The *Esprit des Lois*, sprawling, curious, and unbalanced as it was, was to prove one of the most influential works of the eighteenth century" (ibid.).

11. *The Spirit of Laws*, Bk. XXI, ch. 6. In *A History of Modern France*, vol. 1: 1715-1799 (New York: Pelican Books, 1961), p. 166, the author, Alfred Cobban, says that "the idea of the separation of powers, incorrectly attributed to Montesquieu, who had argued for a balance and not a rigid separation, was employed to exclude executive influence from the legislature; on the other hand, the principle of popular sovereignty justified the legislative assembly in any invasion of the sphere of the executive."

8

Religion and Tolerance

Tolerance in matters of religious belief was a subject of consuming interest and concern to the great eighteenth-century thinkers and writers. Voltaire, Montesquieu, Helvétius, d'Holbach, Turgot, and Condorcet all expressed themselves on a problem that had corroded French life since the sixteenth century.

Their common concern was no coincidence. The memory of the religious wars, the inhumanity and divisiveness of the continuing persecution of the Protestants, the repressive and oppressive domination of the Catholic Church exercising a religious monopoly with state approval, the corruption and ignorance of so many of its clergy, all weighed heavily on the minds of the philosophes. They shared the same conviction that the problem had to be addressed and solved. Their differences were in their approach to the problem and in the emphasis they gave to their proposed solutions.

For example, Montesquieu's critique and suggested remedy was by means of an indirect, delicate, and very gentle presentation and proposal. In letter 85 of the *Persian Letters,* Uzbek says to Mirza:

It is no use to say that it is not in the king's interest to allow more than one religion in the state. Even if every religion in the world gathered together there it would not do him any harm, since every single one of them commands obedience and preaches respect for authority.

I admit that the history books are full of religious wars; but it should be carefully noted that these wars are not produced by the fact that there is more than one religion, but by the spirit of intolerance, urging on the one which believed itself to be dominant.[1]

Voltaire handled the subject of intolerance lightly, on occasion, and usually with wit and satire. In his *Letters on the English,* as previously noted, he contrasted English tolerance of religious differences with French intolerance.[2] Of the English, he said in Letter 5, "This is a land of sects. An Englishman, like a free man, goes to heaven by whatever route he chooses." In the same letter he stressed the differences in morals between the English and the French clergy:

When [the English] learn that in France young men known for their debauches and raised to the prelacy by intrigues, compose tender songs, give long and exquisite dinners almost every day . . . and call themselves "the successors of the Apostles," they thank God that they are Protestants.

In Letter 6, he made this observation:

If there were just one religion in England, despotism would threaten; if there were two religions, they would cut each other's throats; but there are thirty religions, and they live together peacefully and happily.

His mood was different when he wrote the *Traité sur tolerance* (Treatise on tolerance). He was then engaged in a crusade to reverse the verdict in the Calas case. Calas, it may be recalled, was the unfortunate Protestant who was tried, convicted, tortured, and executed in Toulouse on the specious charge that he had murdered his own son to prevent his conversion to Catholicism.

In a very serious state of mind, Voltaire urged tolerance for Protestants. While admitting that they, too, had been intolerant, he recommended a relatively modest political program of allowing the Huguenots to return to France with permission to worship freely. In that context he said:

> Do I propose then, that every citizen shall be free to follow his reason, and believe whatever his enlightened or deluded reason shall dictate to him? Certainly, provided he does not disturb the public order. . . . If you insist it is a crime not to believe in the dominant religion, you condemn the first Christians, your forefathers . . . and you justify those whom you reproach for persecuting them.

He concluded that men "disturb society when they engender fanaticism. Hence, men must avoid fanaticism in order to deserve toleration."[3]

Claude Adrien Helvétius (1715–1771) and Paul Henri Thiry, Baron d'Holbach (1723–1789), were unusual contributors to eighteenth-century French thought in that both were millionaires as well as philosophes. They, like the other philosophes, were critics of the very system that had provided the means for the accumulation of their wealth. Helvétius, in fact, acquired his fortune as the result of his appointment, through influence at the court, to the profitable position of *fermier-général* or collector of taxes.[4] Although neither church nor state had been unkind to them, each was a more severe critic of the religious, political, and social structure of eighteenth-century France than either Montesquieu or Voltaire.

Helvétius wrote two books that stated his philosophic views. The first of them, entitled *De l'Esprit* (On intelligence) was published in 1758, and shortly thereafter, became the victim of a celebrated act of suppression that served to make it a best seller.[5] Initially it had received the stamp of approval of the censor, Jean Pierre Tercier. Shortly thereafter the Council of State revoked the privilege to print and Tercier was removed from his post, despite Helvétius's protest that he had not attacked Christianity. A few months later, in January 1759, the pope condemned the book and in February of that year it was publicly burned pursuant to an order issued by the parliament. Helvétius escaped imprisonment in the Bastille by making a humiliating retraction, as previously noted, but was nevertheless punished by the sentence of confinement to his estate for a period of two years.

His second book, *De l'Homme* (On man),[6] was published posthumously in 1772, a postponement undoubtedly caused by the well-founded fear that publication would be followed by censorship and punishment. *On Man* was a hard, stinging attack on religious intolerance and the cruelty, inhumanity, and repression that had been engendered in the name of religion. "Religious intolerance," he said, "is the daughter of sacerdotal ambition and stupid credulity."[7] Amplifying that view of religious intolerance, he said:

> If I believe my nurse and my tutor, every other religion is false, mine alone is the truth. But is it acknowledged such by the universe? No, the earth still groans under the multitude of temples consecrated to error.[8] . . .
>
> What does the history of religion teach us? That they have

everywhere lighted up the torch of intolerance, strewed the plains with corpses, imbrued the fields with blood, burned cities and laid waste empires.[9]

On the relationship between religion and education, he was equally critical:

In every religion the first objective of the priest is to stifle the curiosity of man, to prevent the examination of every dogma whose absurdity is too palpable to be concealed.[10] . . .

The power of the priest depends upon the superstitions and stupid credulity of the people. It is of little worth to him that they be learned; the less they know the more docile they will be to his dictates.[11]

Accordingly he advocated the reduction of the power of the church in France, the complete divorce of church and state in matters of education, and the rebuilding of the entire educational system in France by the transfer of control from the church to the state.

D'Holbach, described by the Durants as "the best loved of all the philosophes in Paris,"[12] was also the most radical of them in his views on the subject of religion. He was the atheist among them, called by some of his contemporaries "the personal enemy of the Almighty."[13]

He was also a man of such sterling qualities of character, so gentle, generous, and kind in his relations with people, that he was a persuasive example that religious belief is not a necessary condition for conduct that is moral, any more than it is an assurance of morality in conduct. He was a gracious, hospitable host whose home became a favorite meeting place for the intelligentsia, including Turgot and Condorcet. His performance as a host also earned for him the unsolicited and unaccredited honorary title of "*le premier maitre d'hotel de la philosophia.*"[14]

D'Holbach's accomplishments included notable erudition, especially in the field of science. In recognition of the scope of his learning, he was invited to contribute articles to the *Encyclopédie* on various aspects of science and, beginning in 1752, he actually contributed about four hundred articles dealing with a wide variety of scientific subjects.

Part of his hostility toward the Catholic Church can be attributed to his conviction that its control of education was an impediment to the acquisition and development of scientific knowledge. But it is likely that his uncompromising opposition to all organized religion was also a reaction of his innate kindness and his humanitarian sensitivity, which were revolted by religion's history of intolerance, prejudice, persecution, and strife, and the cruelty and suffering that had been inflicted upon people in its name. Another factor in the formation of his point of view was his analysis of the historical record, which showed that the Catholic Church generally had supported tyrannical governments in order to maintain its own dominance.

At least five tracts attributable to him were written between 1761 and 1770, all of them devoted to his crusade against organized religion in general and the Catholic Church and clergy in particular.[15] The word "attributable" is used advisedly, since the dangers inherent in censorship, *lettres de cachet*, imprisonment, and consignment to service in the galleys necessitated underground methods of publication including printing in Amsterdam and surreptitious importation into France using various pseudonyms.

D'Holbach's *Système de la nature, ou des Lois due monde, physique et du monde moral* (System of nature, or the laws of the physical and moral world) was published in 1770. In this work, he advocated abolition of all doctrines that inhibited human happiness and freedom, and he proposed a new society based on atheistic materialism and governed by enlightened men. Because of these radical and iconoclastic ideas, the book's authorship and source of publication had to be carefully concealed.

Ostensibly the book was printed in London. But in fact it was printed in Amsterdam. Its authorship was attributed to a man named Mirabaud, who had died ten years before publication. No one believed that it had been written by the dead Mirabaud, but, fortunately for d'Holbach, the few men who were privy to his secret kept silent until after he had died. Of course the fact that the book had to be brought into France by clandestine means stimulated the appetite for reading it, and *Système de la nature* became another eighteenth-century best seller.

Another stimulant to circulation was the almost automatic and quite predictable reaction of church and state to the book's appearance in France. The quadrennial Assembly of the Clergy, Louis XVI, and the parliament of Paris were of one mind regarding d'Holbach's *Système de la nature*. The unanimous verdict was suppression and penalty was based on the charge that it was "impious, blasphemous, seditious, tending to destroy all idea of divinity, to rouse the people to revolt against religion and government, to overthrow all the principles of public security and morality and to turn subjects away from obedience to their sovereign." The consequent sentence was a directive to burn the book, arrest the author, and inflict appropriate punishment.

While d'Holbach's *Système*, with its advocacy of atheism, did not arouse among the philosophes the violent antipathy that was stirred among the leaders of the establishment, the book did meet with the disapproval of some of the philosophes, most of whom were either deists or theists.[16] Voltaire, the standard-bearer of the philosophes, expressed his disapproval in a charming way, designed to make a point without offense. In his article on God in the *Philosophical Dictionary*, he addressed d'Holbach's views on the existence of God:

> I am persuaded that you are in a great error, but I am equally confident that you are honest in your self-delusion. . . . Everywhere you inspire probity. The philosophic dispute will only be between you and a few philosophers scattered over Europe and the rest of the world will not even hear of it. The people do not read us. . . . You are wrong, but we owe respect to your genius and your virtue.[17]

Voltaire's views on religion at first glance seem somewhat ambivalent. Early in his career he was an impassioned foe of the established church. But late in his life he built a small chapel near his home at Ferney, which he claimed was "the only church in the world dedicated to God alone; all others are dedicated to saints."[18] His position in his later years can be summed up as deistic and tolerant or, as he said very simply, "for God and toleration."[19] Apparently, he feared that support of atheism would imperil the cause of religious toleration. Nevertheless, some of his companions in arms, in the campaign against the dominance of the church and its subjection of the human spirit, came to regard Voltaire as a leader who had lost his way on this subject.

A careful analysis of his religious views, however, will reveal that he did not depart from a prior conviction or position. The difference was that toward the end of his life, the heat of controversy had diminished and the expression of his position on religion lacked the stridency of the battle cry of prior years—the famous "écrasez l'infâme" (crush the infamy).[20] The infamy, in Voltaire's view, was not belief in a Supreme Being, a belief to which he subscribed and consistently adhered. Rather, it was the religious establishment and the inequities perpetrated in the name of the church.

Three events inspired the campaign to "crush the infamy":

The first was an edict adopted in 1759, following an attempt to assassinate the king. At the insistence of the French clergy, one of its provisions stated that any attack upon the church was a crime to be punished by death. The philosophes saw this as a "declaration of war."[21]

The second was the Calas case of 1762, in which, it will be recalled, Jean Calas, a Protestant, was charged, tried, convicted, tortured, and executed on the spurious ground that he had murdered his son to prevent him from becoming a Catholic. As a further punishment for that alleged crime, his property was confiscated and his family was persecuted.

The third event, also occurring in 1762, was the burning in Paris and again in Geneva of Rousseau's *Emile*.

The king's counsel, Maître Omer Joly de Fleury, demanded before the Paris parliament that the book be suppressed on the ground that it was Rousseau's objective "to destroy the truth of Sacred Scripture and the prophesies, the certitude of the miracles described in the Holy Books, the infallibility of revelation and the authority of the Church." The parliament thereupon directed that the book be torn up and burned, and "that all those who have copies of the book shall deliver them . . . to be destroyed . . . ; that all sellers or distributors thereof shall be arrested and punished . . . ;" and that "J.J. Rousseau shall be apprehended and brought to the Conciergerie prison of the Palace."[22]

The Geneva condemnation of *Emile* also directed the burning of *The Social Contract* on the ground that both books were "impious, scandalous, bold, full of blasphemies and calumnies against religion."[23] It was then that Voltaire, incensed by these outrages, coined the slogan "*écrasez l'infâme*" and launched his campaign to crush the infamy of persecutions, censorship, torture, the propagation of superstition, and the church's control of education as well.

One sentence in Voltaire's *Dictionnaire philosophique* on the subject of superstition is almost a summation of the essence of his continuing judgment about the fundamental meaning of religion. He said there, that "almost everything that goes beyond the adoration of a Supreme Being and of submitting one's heart to his eternal orders, is superstition."[24]

Whereas Voltaire challenged traditional dogma from the point of view of an independent-minded outsider, his comrade Turgot spent much of his life as an insider, beginning his career as a spokesman for the conservative religious establishment. As previously noted, Turgot's early life was devoted to preparation for a career in the church. At the age of nineteen he had become Abbé de Brucourt. In 1750, at the age of twenty-three, in his capacity as a prior of the Sorbonne, he delivered a lecture at the Sorbonne called "The Advantages That the Establishment of Christianity Has Conferred upon the Human Race," in which he argued that the "Christian religion alone has . . . brought to light the rights of humanity."[25]

Three years later he wrote two letters on the subject of tolerance—*Lettres sur la tolérance*. In the intervening years he had decided not to pursue a religious career and his point of view had changed. The abbé had become a philosophe.

When Turgot was being considered by Louis XVI for the critical office of comptroller-general his reputation for independence in thinking and the record of his infrequent attendance at mass had preceded him. Louis XVI was counselled by the religious advisers at court that Turgot was a nonbeliever and, therefore, disqualified, despite his record as an incorruptible and outstandingly able administrator.

To Turgot, toleration in matters of religious belief and practices was not an academic issue. During his term of office as comptroller-general he submitted a memoir to the king urging the adoption of a policy of toleration. Although it did not accomplish an immediate result, due to the opposition of the Assembly of Clergy, it planted a seed which came to fruition in 1787, too late to stem the advance of the rising storm. The Edict of Toleration, issued that year, "granted the Protestants civil rights, including those of entry into various hitherto prohibited trades and professions, and recognized the legitimacy of Protestant marriages registered with the local authorities."[26]

The philosophes' aim of achieving religious toleration was only a part of a broader program, the goal of which was not only freedom in religious belief and practice, but freedom embracing people as social beings in the widest sense. The philosophes hoped to wrest away from religious and secular authority all the restraints imposed upon the minds of people in matters temporal as well as religious. The shared objective was the achievement of both political and religious freedom and, equally important, tolerance for differences in opinion and belief. In his felicitous way, Voltaire summed up the rationale for tolerance in one pithy, sparkling sentence: "In politics as in religion, toleration is a necessity."

Notes

1. Montesquieu, *Persian Letters*, trans. C. J. Betts (New York: Penguin Classics, 1973), p. 165.

2. *Lettres sur les Anglais*, also entitled *Lettres philosophique*.

3. *Selected Works*, ed. Joseph McCabe (London, 1911), pp. 100, 108.

4. Helvétius's father was physician to the queen.

5. Twenty editions were printed in France and the book was translated into English and German editions.

6. The full title was *De l'Homme, de ses facultés intellectuelles, et de son eduction* (A treatise on man: His intellectual faculties and his education).

7. *On Man,* VII, i.

8. Ibid., I, ii.

9. Ibid., VII, i.

10. Ibid., II, xxii.

11. Ibid., I, ix.

12. W. and A. Durant, *The Age of Voltaire,* vol. 9 of *The Story of Civilization* (New York: Simon and Schuster, 1965), p. 695.

13. P. Edwards, ed., *The Encyclopedia of Philosophy* (New York: Free Press, 1973), vol. 4, p. 49.

14. W. and A. Durant, *The Age of Voltaire,* p. 703.

15. The most important of these tracts, known to have been written by d'Holbach, are the following: *Le Christianisme dévoilé, ou Examen des principes et des effets de la religion chrétienne* (1761); *Théologia portative, ou Dictionnaire a brégé de la religion chrétienne* (1767); *La contagion sacrée, ou Histoire naturelle de la superstition* (1768); *Lettres à Eugénie, ou Préseratif contre les préjugés* (1768); and *Histoire critique de Jesus-Christ, ou Analyse raisonné des Evangiles* (177).

16. *Webster's New World Dictionary of the American Language,* rev. ed., ed. David B. Guralnik (New York: Warner Books, 1987), provides the following simple definitions of deism and theism: Deism is defined as "the doctrine that God created the world and its natural laws, but takes no further part in its functioning." Theism is defined as "belief in a god or gods" or "belief in one God who is creator and ruler of the world."

17. See W. and A. Durant, *The Age of Voltaire,* pp. 712–13.

18. See W. and A. Durant, *The Age of Voltaire,* p. 751.

19. Ibid., p. 752.

20. That expression appears in a letter written by Voltaire to d'Alembert on November 28, 1762. It is part of the following sentence

in that letter: "*Qui que vous passiez, écrasez l'infâme, et aimez que vous aime.*" (Whatever you do, crush the infamy, and love those who love you.)

21. W. and A. Durant, *The Age of Voltaire*, p. 737.

22. *Collection Complète*, IXa, pp. v-x. See W. and A. Durant, *Rousseau and Revolution*, vol. 10 of *The Story of Civilization* (New York: Simon and Schuster, 1967), p. 190.

23. *Collection*, IXb, 4.

24. From his article on "Superstition." See W. and A. Durant, *The Age of Voltaire*, p. 738.

25. See W. and A. Durant, *Rousseau and Revolution*, p. 77.

26. Alfred Cobban, *A History of Modern France*, vol. 1: 1715-1799 (New York: Penguin, 1961), p. 109.

9

Intellectual and Historical Inheritance— Summation

Born into the mainstream of French thought in the Age of Enlightenment, Condorcet was the inheritor of the intellectual currents that have been briefly sketched in the preceding section. Before his birth in 1743 Voltaire had already published his *Letters on the English* and had become the ardent advocate in France of Newton and Locke. And Montesquieu had already published the *Persian Letters.* Condorcet was only four when Diderot was engaged as editor-in-chief of the *Encyclopédie,* just five when Montesquieu published *The Spirit of Laws,* eight years old when volume one of the *Encyclopédie* was published, a boy of twelve when Rousseau published the *Discourse on the Origins and Foundations of Inequality among Men,* and had not yet attained his majority when Rousseau, then aged fifty, published *The Social Contract* in 1762. In 1765, Condorcet, at the age of twenty-two, had his first encounter[1] with one of the intellectual leaders of France—the renowned d'Alembert, one of the great men of the Enlightenment, with whom he shortly established the relationship of protégé and friend.

As a citizen of France, he was well aware of his nation's historical record during the sixteenth and seventeenth centuries, which included such egregious events as the Wars of Religion, the massacre of St. Bartholomew's Day, the revocation of the Edict of Nantes by Louis XIV, and the consequent unhappy departure into exile of 200,000 Huguenots, reminiscent of the biblical exodus from Egypt. That record was also replete with many other instances of the abuse of power, past and present, by the deliberate creation and use of a pervasive sense of fear as a matter of policy. The objective of the policy—the exercise of control over the minds and persons of potential mavericks and malcontents and, if necessary, their suppression or elimination—was accomplished through such instruments of persecution as censorship, *lettres de cachet,* and arrest and imprisonment in the Bastille, without notice or an opportunity to be heard.

To the historical consciousness of past atrocities and injustices was added the painful awareness in the present of the fundamentally flawed character of the life of the individual in France— the overbearing presence of despotic government, the pervasive climate of intolerance, both political and religious, and the stifling atmosphere of thought control by state and church, which made the expression of nonconformist ideas a perilous adventure and publication a dangerous transgression against the establishment, to be conducted only by concealment and subterfuge.

It was a fortuitous circumstance that Condorcet was born in 1743. By that accident of birth he was destined to be not only the last of the philosophes but the only one to become a participant in the French Revolution and the author of the last testament of the Age of Enlightenment.[2] He was able thereby to bring to the Revolution some measure of the philosophes' devotion to the life of reason and to posterity, the voice of one who had witnessed the Age of Reason and was a fervent advocate of its message.

Thus Condorcet, at the age of twenty-two, braced by these memories, stood at the threshold of his career and faced the future, fortunately unaware that in only twenty-four years he would be thrust into the maelstrom of the Revolution, not just as the only surviving philosophe, but as the only one actively involved in its frenzied and dangerous political life—a sometimes singular voice of reason, compassion, and tolerance in a wilderness of reckless and intemperate passion.

Between 1765 when he made his debut with his *Essay on Integral Calculus* and 1794 when his life ended in a prison cell at Bourg-La-Reine, there were three chapters in Condorcet's life. The first was the period of twenty-five years from 1765 to the beginning of the French Revolution in 1789, during which he made his reputation as an intellectual and earned the status of a philosophe. The second period covered the five years from 1789 to 1793 when, as the last of the philosophes, he was an active member of several of the revolutionary assemblies. The third chapter, the last year of his life, was the fevered period during which he wrote his testament to posterity—the *Sketch*.

Notes

1. J. Salwyn Shapiro, in *Condorcet and the Rise of Liberalism* (New York: Octagon Books, 1963), says that Condorcet "became deeply interested in mathematics, and at the age of sixteen, he brilliantly defended a mathematical thesis before a body of mathematicians, among whom was d'Alembert."

2. Among the cast of brilliant thinkers who died before Condorcet were Montesquieu in 1755, Helvétius in 1771, Voltaire and Rousseau in 1778, Turgot in 1781, d'Alembert in 1783, Diderot in 1784, and d'Holbach in 1789.

Part Three

Condorcet the Man—
Friends, Marriage, and His Works
Before the Revolution (1765–1789)

10

Introduction

The society in which Condorcet lived was filled with bright people brimming with ideas for the improvement of the human condition. Their outlook was broadly humanitarian, and they were buoyed by confidence in the power of reason and optimism about the future.

This was a period of renaissance, inspired not by the rediscovery of the Greek and Roman past, which had been the impetus for the Great Renaissance of the fourteenth through seventeenth centuries, but by the vision of a future of freedom. Petrarch (1304–1374) thought of the future as a time when, "after the darkness has been dispelled, our grandsons will be able to walk into the pure radiance of the past." The brilliant minds with whom Condorcet associated between 1765 and 1789 thought of the future, to faintly paraphrase Petrarch, as a time when the darkness of oppression and intolerance would be dispelled and their descendants would walk into a radiant future of freedom. The world they envisioned would be one in which despotism would be stamped out and the people would be the

119

sovereigns rather than the subjects. The inevitable consequence would be the recognition that people "are born free and equal and have certain natural, essential and inalienable rights, among which may be reckoned the right of enjoying and defending their lives and liberties . . . and of seeking and obtaining their safety and happiness."[1]

It is surprising that the Marquis de Condorcet, the aristocrat who was a democrat by conviction, quickly moved into the very center of this circle of witty intellectuals and that he was quickly accepted by them. His family background, education, and temperament conspired to make him an unlikely candidate for admission to this clique of progressives who were socially at ease in the brilliant life of Parisian salons. His personality did not quite fit into a society of people who were at once serious and gay, able to exchange weighty ideas while taking part in quick and witty repartee and flirtatious badinage.

As a child Condorcet was sickly. His doting, overly protective mother resorted to an unusual method of trying to protect him from rough play with other children: she dressed him in the clothes of a girl until he was nine. The embarrassment and ridicule to which he was subjected were sufficient to damage his self-esteem and contribute to both shyness and timidity.

As noted before, Condorcet's father, an army officer, died when he was an infant, so he was brought up in a household lacking a male role model. His mother was intensely religious, and a paternal uncle, who was a bishop, supervised his education, first in a Jesuit preparatory school at Rheims and then at the Jesuit College of Navarre in Paris. It is remarkable that, although he was raised in an environment dominated by religious and aristocratic influences, far removed from the prevailing winds of the reformative thought of the philosophes, he became one of them soon after his arrival in Paris.

When he announced that he had decided to pursue the career of a mathematician, he encountered strong opposition from members of his family, who were steeped in the tradition that the army or the clergy was the only suitable career for an aristocrat. So intense was their disapproval of his choice that they opposed his admission to the Academy of Sciences and successfully delayed his acceptance as a member. It is a tribute to an underlying strength of character, combined with the need for self-expression and independence in thinking, that Condorcet resisted these entreaties and left for Paris to pursue the career he had selected.

He settled in the city in 1762 at the age of nineteen, using an allowance given to him by a loving mother. He continued his studies in mathematics and in 1765 produced his first major work, the "Essay on Integral Calculus," which, as mentioned in the preface, attracted the attention and the admiration of d'Alembert and led to his introduction by d'Alembert to Julie de Lespinasse and her salon.

The timidity, the shyness, and the social awkwardness of this tall, thin, stoop-shouldered, very serious young aristocrat were overlooked because he gave promise of outstanding intellectual achievement in the field of mathematics.[2] On further acquaintance and more profound analysis of the inner man, Julie de Lespinasse was moved to say that he was "second only to d'Alembert in the range of his intellect, and perhaps above him in the warmth of his benevolence."

Condorcet continued for a time to study and write on the subject of mathematics. The importance of the contributions he made in this field was recognized by his election in 1769, when he was only twenty-six, to membership in the Academy of Science. At this point in his life "the range of his intellect" broadened. The stimulation of contact with many of the fine minds of the time through his admission to salon society and the Academy of Science,[3] expanded his vision, so that while mathematics continued to be a subject of interest, it was thereafter a subordinate one.

From that time forward his interests were catholic in their scope. He immersed himself in study and thought, and wrote about a wide range of scientific, political, social, and economic issues. He also produced works of a literary character. The full extent of his application to these projects can be judged by the fact that the first edition of his collected works, published in 1804, ten years after his death, filled twenty-one volumes.[4] This prodigious mental activity was more than an exhibition of industry. The resulting product was excellent in quality.

In recognition of his achievements, he was appointed secretary of the Academy of Science in 1777. In that capacity, Condorcet followed the practice that had been adopted by the remarkable Fontanelle,[5] who wrote memorials for departed members of the French Academy. These memorials, called *éloges*, covered the lives and works of eminent scientists of the eighteenth century and, collectively, constituted a comprehensive picture of contemporary scientific knowledge. Condorcet's efforts in the writing of the *éloges* led to an encyclopedic familiarity with eighteenth-century scientific development and earned for him the high praise of Voltaire. They so impressed Voltaire that he told Condorcet "The public wishes that an Academician might die every week or so that you might have a chance to write about him."[6]

Notes

1. From the Constitution of Massachusetts of 1780, drafted by John Adams.

2. See chapter 12 and also J. S. Schapiro, *Condorcet and the Rise*

of Liberalism (New York: Octagon Books, Inc., 1963), p. 68.

3. Among the men he met were Voltaire, Helvétius, Lafayette, Franklin, and Turgot, who became an intimate friend.

4. A later edition, edited by Condorcet's daughter and M. F. Arago, fills twelve volumes (Paris 1847–1849).

5. Bernard Le Bovier de Fontanelle (1657-1757), a nephew of Corneille, was secretary of the Academy from 1699 to 1741 and lived to the extraordinary age of 100.

6. W. and A. Durant, *Rousseau and Revolution*, vol. 10 of *The Story of Civlization* (New York: Simon and Schuster, 1967), p. 894.

11

d'Alembert

Jean Le Rond l'Alembert (1717–1783), one of the great intellectual leaders of eighteenth-century France, occupies a very special place in the life of Condorcet. When the young Condorcet had the good fortune to meet him and become his protégé, d'Alembert exercised a friendly and powerful influence, both as mentor and advocate, in the development and advancement of Condorcet's career.

The circumstances of d'Alembert's birth and upbringing were anything but auspicious and suggested no promise of greatness to come. He started life as an illegitimate, unwanted, and abandoned baby. His mother, Madame de Tencin, the "chair" of one of the influential salons of Paris, regarded the birth of her son as an impediment to her careers of mistress and *salonnière*. Accordingly she immediately abandoned him at birth on the steps of the baptistry of Saint Jean-Le-Rond, a circumstance that is reflected in the name by which he is known. He was found by the Paris police a few hours after his birth, was baptized by them Jean Baptiste Le Rond, and then sent to a nurse in the country.

His father, the Chevalier Destouches, an artillery general, who had less concern than Mme. Tencin about the effect of the child's birth on his career, claimed his son upon his return from the provinces. For reasons unknown, the Chevalier gave his son the name of d'Arembert, a name that Jean later changed to d'Alembert. The Chevalier's next move was to place the boy in the care of a Mme. Rousseau, the wife of a glazier. The choice was a good one, for she proved to be an excellent mother. The boy flourished in her care, remaining in her home like a devoted son until 1765, when he was a mature and renowned man of forty-eight.

Jean was a model child with a precocious intelligence, so much so that the Chevalier proudly displayed him to Mme. de Tencin when he was seven years old. She was unmoved, however, and exhibited no interest in him, nor did she contribute anything to his support. When the Chevalier died in 1726, he left his son, then nine, an annuity of twelve hundred livres, somewhere in the neighborhood of $2000 in American money.

However, the Destouches family continued its interest in the boy and placed him in the Jansenist College de Mazarin. Subsequently he attended law school for two years, changed from the study of law to the study of medicine, and then abandoned that to pursue his intense interest in mathmatics. This subject became his true métier and the anchor of his subsequent career as a mathematician, scientist, philosopher, writer, co-editor with Diderot of the *Encyclopédie,* and a leading figure of the Enlightenment. His contributions to science include the solution of problems in physics and astronomy.[1] Among his works of philosophy and literature are the many articles written for the *Encyclopédie* and, of course, the introduction to the first volume of the *Encyclopédie,* entitled *Discours préliminaire,* a task for which he was chosen because of his standing as a scientist and his reputation as a writer.

The abandoned baby had become one of the leading intellectuals of the eighteenth century, recognized as a man of distinction by his election to membership in the Academy of Sciences in 1743 and the French Academy in 1754, and becoming its permanent secretary in 1772. Also indicative of his distinguished status was the invitation of Frederick the Great to d'Alembert to become president of the Berlin Academy and the invitation by Catherine the Great to come to Russia and the Academy of St. Petersburg.[2]

This was the man who recognized the superior qualities of Condorcet's mind and chose to become his mentor. According to some historians, Condorcet first encountered d'Alembert when he was sixteen years old on the occasion of his "brilliant" defense of a mathematical thesis before a body of mathematicians, one of whom was d'Alembert.[3] While that assertion may be clouded by some doubt, it is certain that at twenty-one Condorcet did come to the attention of the forty-seven-year-old d'Alembert in 1764, as the result of a paper written by Condorcet dealing with a problem in calculus. At that time d'Alembert and a colleague reported to the Academy of Sciences that "in our view, this paper of M. le marquis de Condorcet reveals much knowledge and insight into the infinitesmal calculus, and we regard it as worthy of publication in the collection of papers by non-members of the Academy."[4]

That paper and his more extensive work on calculus published in 1765, entitled the *Calcul intégral,* moved a contemporary, Joseph Jerome de Lalande (1732–1807), professor of astronomy at the College de France and director of the Paris Observatory, to say that this work placed Condorcet "among the ten foremost mathematicians in Europe."[5]

Shortly after the publication of *Calcul intégral,* in a fateful example of the mysterious chemistry of human relations, d'Alembert began to play the part of Condorcet's mentor and advocate, thereby launching the younger man on his career as a distinguished philosophe and a personality of influence and power in the life of France before and during the French Revolution. It appears that as early as 1765, d'Alembert had begun to exercise his role as Condorcet's patron by informing Lagrange (1736–1813), one of the eminent eighteenth-century mathematicians and astronomers,[6] that he would soon be receiving a copy of the *Calcul intégral*—"an excellent work in my opinion, and one with which I think you will be very satisfied."[7]

The next, and in its way, perhaps the most important step in the promotion of the career of his protégé came in 1769 when d'Alembert introduced Condorcet to the celebrated salon of Julie de Lespinasse, which flourished from 1764 until her death in 1776. The salon on the rue de Belle Chasse was a vital center of the cultural life of Paris, alive with the exciting exchange of new ideas, a meeting place for leaders of the revolution in thinking, and, as one writer put it, the "antechamber to the French Academy."[8]

The price of admission was intellectual status and Condorcet's acceptance was a certification that he had achieved the position of an intellectual worthy of participation in the charmed circle. He had achieved that station not only by writing the *Calcul intégral* but also by the mathematical and scientific works that followed it dealing with the application of calculus to the solution of problems created by Newtonian physics.[9]

In 1770 Julie de Lespinasse did Condorcet a great service by arranging a meeting with Voltaire. This meeting came about inadvertently through d'Alembert, who was suffering from an illness, probably psychological and depressive in character. "Dr." Lespinasse prescribed a vacation for d'Alembert and conscripted Condorcet to accompany him. The two men journeyed to Ferney,[10] on the French-Swiss border, near Geneva, where Voltaire had established his home in 1759 and where he continued to live until 1778. There they stayed for two weeks while d'Alembert recuperated.

This gave Condorcet, "the last philosophe," an unusual opportunity to spend time with the premier philosophe. Those two weeks, attributable solely to d'Alembert's illness and intimacy with Voltaire, gave Voltaire the time to measure the quality of Condorcet's character and mind and to earn for Condorcet his respect, friendship, and support in the promotion of his career. That friendship is the subject of chapter 13.

As mentioned previously, the recognition of Condorcet's intellectual talent eventually led to his admission to the Academy of Sciences and to the French Academy, both with the active participation and aggressive promotion of d'Alembert. The two academies were created in the seventeenth century during the reign of Louis XIV, "The Grand Monarch," who considered that "buildings were not enough for his glory" and therefore that "all the arts, letters and sciences must come together . . . to glorify his person and his reign."[11] The French Academy (*l'Académie Française*) was charged with the duty of governance of French literature, grammar, spelling, and rhetoric. Membership was limited to forty, who were sometimes called, with a bit of hyperbole, "the forty immortals."[12]

At the time of Condorcet's admissions, d'Alembert was a commanding leader of both institutions. As so frequently happens with organizations, nonpolitical as well as political, the two academies were split between two internal factions with differing points of view and objectives. On the one side were the reformers, the philosophe party led by d'Alembert; their opposition was the court coterie, called the *dévots*. That title is colored with contempt based on the fact that in 1684, the court of Louis XIV, newly installed at Versailles, following the lead of the king, suddenly became devout, leading La Broyère to observe that "a dévot is a man who under an atheist king, would be an atheist."[13]

In the contest between the philosophes and the dévots for control of the two academies, d'Alembert was successful but only after a prolonged struggle that ended with Condorcet's admission to the French Academy in 1782. D'Alembert died a year later, but his work had been done. Condorcet was then ready to fill the leadership role that had been left open by d'Alembert's death.

Nineteen years had gone by since the relationship between protégé and mentor had begun. It had been an enormously productive period in the advancement of Condorcet's career, an indebtedness to which Condorcet paid tribute in his biography of d'Alembert.[14]

Notes

1. Among d'Alembert's many works are the Traité de dynamique (1743); Reflexions sur la cause générale des vents, which won the prize of the Berlin Academy in 1746; Reflexions sur la procession des équinoxes et sur la nutation (1749); Eléments de musique théorique et pratique (1779); eight volumes of Opuscules mathématique (1761–1780). D'Alembert's name is memorialized in a principle of dynamics still called "D'Alembert's Principle," which permitted the reduction of a problem in dynamics to one in statics. Among his other writings is an interesting essay entitled Essai sur la société des gens de lettres et des grands, sur la récompense littéraires, published in 1753 and addressed to the distinctions accorded to men of wealth and high birth as distinguished from those accorded to men of knowledge or talent.

2. D'Alembert declined both invitations. Subsequently, in 1763, Frederick invited d'Alembert to dine with him. That invitation d'Alembert accepted.

3. See J. S. Schapiro, *Condorcet and the Rise of Liberalism* (New York: Octagon Books, 1963), p. 67. Keith M. Baker in *Condorcet: From Natural Philosophy to Social Mathematics* (Chicago: University of Chicago Press, 1982), p. 9, says that "it is not entirely clear . . . when Condorcet first met d'Alembert," and that "the traditional account . . . has not so far been confirmed by direct evidence."

4. Baker, *Condorcet*, pp. 6–7.

5. Ibid., p. 7.

6. Comte Joseph Louis Lagrange was born in Turin of French and Italian descent. Before he was twenty he was professor of geometry at the royal artillery school at Turin. In 1793 he became president of the commission on weights and measures and was influential in the adoption of the decimal base for the metric system.

7. Baker, *Condorcet*, p. 9.

8. Ibid., p. 23.

9. The *Calcul intégral* was followed in 1766 by a study of the "three-body problem" and in 1768 by a more general essay on the application of integral calculus to Newtonian physics (ibid., p. 8). The "three-body problem" is a problem in celestial mechanics involving the study of the motions of celestial bodies as they move under the influence of their mutual gravitation. The calculation of such motions is complicated when more than two bodies are involved.

10. Voltaire's presence in Ferney is memorialized in the town's present name—Ferney Voltaire.

11. Pierre Goubert, *Louis XIV and the Twenty Million Frenchmen* (New York: Vintage Books, 1972), p. 81.

12. Robin Briggs in *Early Modern France 1560-1715* (Oxford: Oxford University Press, 1977), p. 196, goes so far as to say that the salons became "more significant than the official academies."

13. Pierre Goubert, *Louis XIV and the Twenty Million Frenchmen*, p. 157.

14. *Éloge de M. d'Alembert.*

12

Julie de Lespinasse

Julie Jeanne Eléonore de Lespinasse began life with the same handicap as d'Alembert. She was the illegitimate daughter of the Comtesse d'Albon and Gaspard de Vichy, brother of Mme. du Deffand, one of the great eighteenth-century *salonnières*. Like d'Alembert she overcame that handicap and, in the course of her short life (1732–1776), she became a distinguished leader of a very celebrated salon and, in her own right, something of a literary figure; her name and achievements are still remembered in twentieth-century encyclopedias.[1]

The early life of Mme. de Lespinasse had something of a Cinderella quality. Her mother, unlike d'Alembert's, cared for her and acknowledged her as her daughter. The comtesse d'Albon brought Julie up with her other children, gave her an excellent education, and would have legitimized her, except for the objection of a "wicked" half-sister, who didn't want Julie to share in the family fortune.

When Julie was sixteen. the Comtesse died and at that age, without the protection of her mother, she was vulnerable and subservient, and was forced to live with her hostile sister, not as a sister, but in the capacity of a retainer serving as a governess for the sister's children. In that position she was so unhappy that she decided to take a room in a convent as a boarder. At that point Mme. du Deffand, the sister of Julie's father, proposed that Julie should come to live with her. After considerable hesitation she accepted that offer and joined Mme. du Deffand in 1754 at age twenty-two.

Marie de Vichy-Chamrond, Marquise du Deffand (1697–1780), was then fifty-four and blind. Once a famous beauty, noted for her brilliant mind and wit, she had presided for many years over a salon rivalled only by those of Mme. de Tencin and Mme. Geoffrin. Probably the victim of glaucoma, she turned to Julie to assist her in the conduct of her salon. For ten years, from 1754 to 1764, that was a function that Julie fulfilled with great intelligence and charm.

Then in 1764 a serious rupture took place in the relations of the two women, the unintentional cause of which was d'Alembert. Mme. du Deffand had first met him in 1743 and was enormously impressed by his intelligence. Although she was twenty years his senior in age, a close and warm friendship developed between them, and he was a constant presence at her salon. When Julie entered Mme du Deffand's salon as her assistant, d'Alembert was almost immediately attracted to her because of the "electric affinity" between them, an affinity based on the fact that they were both born illegitimate.[2] Their relationship appears to have been platonic but it was deep and abiding and when Julie died in 1776 at the age of forty-four, d'Alembert was shattered.[3]

In the meantime the blind Mme. du Deffand sensed the growing attachment between Julie and d'Alembert. Ultimately, suppressed jealousy and disappointment exploded. Mme. du Deffand accused Julie of deceiving her. Feeling her position to be untenable in that atmosphere, Julie left in May 1764 and established her own salon in the rue de Belle Chasse. Mme. du Deffand made the mistake at that point of insisting that d'Alembert make a choice between her and Julie. Faced with that ultimatum, d'Alembert chose to terminate his relationship with her and join Julie in her salon.

Kenneth Clark made the shrewd observation that "the success of the Parisian salons depended very largely on the fact that the court and government were not situated in Paris, but in Versailles."[4] That is true. But because Versailles seemed to be very far away in "a separate world,"[5] the salons needed a spark to light them, and that was contributed by the *salonnières*. Their dynamic personalities energized influential circles of people and made a unique contribution to civilization.

The salon that Julie established was an immediate and continuing success. She was bright, tactful, skillful in leading conversations, and endowed with charm and a warm personality— a combination of qualities that attracted distinguished people, women as well as men, and made her salon so notable that it has been described as "the most in vogue, the most eagerly frequented [salon], at an epoch that counted so many that were brilliant."[6]

Because of his provincial family upbringing and doting mother, as noted earlier, Condorcet was shy, awkward, introverted, and very serious when he was introduced to the salon of Julie de Lespinasse. Even his physical appearance contributed to the aura of diffidence and insecurity. He was described as a "tall youth, awkward, timid, and embarrassed, who walked with a stoop and bit his nails, who was silent or spoke rapidly in a low voice, inclining his head and blushing."[7]

Beneath that shield of shyness, Julie, an excellent judge of character, recognized in the young man introduced to her by d'Alembert, a splendid intelligence and a fine character. This is how she described him in her discerning way:

> He has received from nature the loftiest mind, the most considerable talent and the fairest of souls; his talent would have been enough to make him famous, his mind to make him sought after; but his soul wins him friendship of all who come to know him at all well.[8]

Despite her acquaintance with so many of the bright minds who attended her salon, Julie was particularly impressed by the mind of Condorcet. In one of her letters she said:

> Converse with him, read what he has written; talk to him of philosophy, belles lettres, sciences, the arts, jurisprudence, and when you have heard him, you will tell yourself a hundred times a day that this is the most astonishing man you have ever heard; he is ignorant of nothing, not even the things most alien to his tastes and occupations; he will know . . . the genealogies of the courtiers, the details of the police and the names of the hats in fashion; in fact, nothing is beneath his attention and his memory is so prodigious that he has never forgotten anything.[9]

Under her gentle tutelage he acquired the social graces and the assurance that together with his fine mind and character made him a leader of reform after the death of d'Alembert. Intellectually, too, Condorcet's interests broadened as a result of his association with Julie's salon and the bright minds who frequented it. Many of these became his close friends, particularly Turgot, another of the great men of eighteenth-century France, who became an intimate friend. Their varied interests—economic, social, political, and literary—undoubtedly exposed his mind to new perspectives. Mathematics continued to be a subject of study, but it was subordinate to others and, in a sense, it became a tool useful in dealing with broad social, economic, and political issues. His forays into these fields are the subject of chapter 17.

Another aspect of Condorcet's character that impressed Mme. de Lespinasse and other contemporaries was the extent to which this essentially gentle man could be aroused to passionate fury by infringements of the fundamental rights of human beings. In one of her letters, she said:

> This soul, calm and moderate in the ordinary course of life, becomes ardent and full of fire when it is a question of defending the oppressed or protecting that which is even more precious, the liberty of men and the virtue of the unfortunate.[10]

Even more revealing of this aspect of Condorcet's personality is the advice he gave in a letter to his daughter shortly before his death. He asked her to preserve "in all its purity and strength the sentiment which makes us sensitive to the pain of all living things. Do not limit yourself to sympathy for human suffering but let that sympathy extend to the suffering of animals."[11]

The "postgraduate schooling" of Condorcet under the tutelage of the perceptive and sympathetic Julie de Lespinasse came to an end on May 23, 1776, when, at the age of forty-four, she died, a victim of tuberculosis. He was then thirty-three, a distinguished philosophe, recognized and respected for the distinction of his mind and character, and well prepared to take over the mantle of d'Alembert.

Notes

1. See, for example, *Benet's Readers Encyclopedia*, 3rd ed. (New York: Harper Collins, 1987).

2. See W. and A. Durant, *Rousseau and Revolution*, vol. 10 of *The Story of Civilization* (New York: Simon and Schuster, 1967), p. 124.

3. Julie loved the Comte de Guibert, to whom she wrote love letters that were fortunately, though curiously, published by Guibert's wife in 1809. They have the literary quality that has earned them a place in *Benet's Readers Encyclopedia*, p. 563.

4. Kenneth Clark, *Civilisation* (New York: Harper and Row, 1969), p. 252.

5. Ibid.

6. This was a characterization by Sainte-Bevre. See W. and A. Durant, *Rousseau and Revolution*, p. 127.

7. L. Cahen, *Condorcet et la Révolution française* (Paris, 1904), p. 5. See J. S. Schapiro, *Condorcet and the Rise of Liberalism* (New York: Octagon Books, 1963), p. 67.

Another description says that "in appearance Condorcet was tall, broad-shouldered, with a rather large head and slender legs." Schapiro, *Condorcet and the Rise of Liberalism*, p. 76.

8. From the *Letters of Julie de Lespinasse*, pp. 232–33. See Keith M. Baker, *Condorcet: From Natural Philosophy to Social Mathematics* (Chicago: University of Chicago Press, 1982), p. 24.

9. From the *Letters of Julie de Lespinasse*, pp. 232–33. See Baker, *Condorcet: From Natural Philosophy to Social Mathematics*, pp. 24–25.

10. See Baker, *Condorcet: From Natural Philosophy to Social Mathematics*, p. 26.

11. See Schapiro, *Condorcet and the Rise of Liberalism*, p. 77.

13

Voltaire

Besides d'Alembert two other men played particularly important roles in Condorcet's life, roles that he celebrated by writing biographies of both of them. The *Life of Turgot* was published in 1786 and the *Life of Voltaire* in 1789, and both were widely read and admired.

Turgot's life and influence on Condorcet will be discussed in the next chapter. Here we will consider the relationship between the young philosophe and the elder statesman of the Enlightenment, which had something of the respect, admiration, and affection of a promising grandson toward an admired grandfather.

Condorcet made the pilgrimage to Ferney[1] in 1770, when he was twenty-seven and Voltaire was seventy-six. Voltaire warmly received the promising young Condorcet as one worthy of admission to the inner circle of accomplished friends, upon whom he bestowed both his approval and affection.

An incident that occurred after the visit to Ferney illustrates the regard and affection that the two men had for each other. Voltaire wrote to Condorcet and asked him to arrange for the publication of an article critical of Montesquieu. Condorcet, feeling that the article should not be printed, wrote a graceful note of declination to Voltaire, saying, "My affection for you causes me to tell you what is best for you, not what would please you. If I loved you less, I would not have the courage to gainsay you." Voltaire was not offended. In a letter that displayed his regard fof Condorcet, as well as his open, lively mind and sense of humor, he said, "One sees always badly when things are far away. We should never blush to go to school even at the age of Methusalah."[2]

Another expression of regard and admiration for Voltaire occurred in connection with Turgot's resignation as comptroller general of finance in 1776. His appointment to that position in 1774 had excited the philosophes and given them great hopes for the promise of reform. When Turgot was forced to resign twenty-two months after his appointment as a result of pressure upon the king by powerful opponents of Turgot's plans, the philosophes were filled with gloom. Condorcet wrote a letter then to Voltaire expressing his deep disappointment and unhappiness about the end of Turgot's effort to accomplish reform. In the course of that letter Condorcet demonstrated the depth of his feeling for Voltaire, saying, "How far we are fallen, my dear and illustrious master, and from such heights."[3]

In another letter to one of his friends, Condorcet described Voltaire as "a great genius" and "the implacable foe of tyranny."[4]

While it is a literary exaggeration, one more expression of esteem deserves mention because it demonstrates the longing for freedom in eighteenth-century France, the popular desire to achieve it that Voltaire had inspired and, incidentally, Condorcet's own estimate of its crucial importance. In his biography of Voltaire, Condorcet captured in one pithy phrase a major contribution of Voltaire to the life of his time. He said, very simply, that but for Voltaire, liberty would have continued to be "a secret among the wise."[5]

Voltaire, for his part, expressed his regard for Condorcet on more than one occasion. In 1772 Condorcet had written a book concerning the lives of eleven academicians of the Academy of Sciences who had died prior to 1699. After he read the book, Voltaire, in a burst of critical enthusiasm, expressed his approval by proclaiming, "This is a king treating the history of his subjects."[6]

One other example of Voltaire's regard for Condorcet warrants mention because it was occasioned by an event that was important in Condorcet's life. When Condorcet became a candidate for admission to the French Academy in 1782 as one of its "forty immortals," Voltaire wrote to Condorcet, "We have need of men in the Academy that think like you."[7]

By that time Condorcet had established an impressive reputation as a mathematician, philosopher, writer, and reformer. Politics, however, played its part even in the supposedly dispassionate decisions of an institution dedicated to the preservation of the purity of the French language. As previously mentioned, there was a division among the members of the Academy that might be characterized as a conservative-liberal split between "the combined forces of the court and clerical groups"[8] and the "Voltaire-d'Alembert group"[9]—a split also described by the more intriguing designation of "dévots" versus "encyclopedists."[10]

With the influential endorsement that had been accorded to him by Voltaire, and the leadership of d'Alembert, Condorcet was elected to membership in the Academy by the narrow margin of one vote, over the court-clerical or dévot candidate, Bailly, a distinguished astronomer.

Notes

1 Voltaire purchased the seigniory of Ferney, near the Swiss border, in 1758.

2. *Correspondence entre Voltaire et Condorcet*, vol. 1, pp. 151–55. See J. S. Schapiro, *Condorcet and the Rise of Liberalism* (New York: Octagon, 1963), pp. 70–71.

3. *Voltaire's Correspondence* (Besterman ed., 19104). See Keith M. Baker, *Condorcet: From Natural Philosophy to Social Mathematics* (Chicago: University of Chicago Press, 1982), p. 73.

4. *Voltaire's Correspondence* (Besterman ed., 16237). See Keith M. Baker, *Condorcet: From Natural Philosophy to Social Mathematics*, p. 32.

5. *Vie de Voltaire*, IV, 182.

6. *Éloges des academiciens de l'Académie royale des Sciences morts depuis l'an 1666 jusqu'en 1699* (Besterman ed., 17159). See Baker, *Condorcet: From Natural Philosophy to Social Mathematics*, p. 38.

7. *Correspondence entre Voltaire et Condorcet*, I, 3, 100–101. See Schapiro, *Condorcet and the Rise of Liberalism*, p. 74.

8. Baker, *Condorcet: From Natural Philosophy to Social Mathematics*, p. 23.

9. Ibid. Voltaire was elected to membership in the French Academy in 1746 and d'Alembert was elected in 1754. He became its permanent secretary in 1772.

10. Baker, *Condorcet: From Natural Philosophy to Social Mathematics*, p. 29.

14

Turgot

Anne Robert Jacques, Baron d'Aulne, known as Turgot, was born in Paris in 1727. In accordance with aristocratic tradition, it was expected and planned that, as a younger son, Turgot's career would be that of the priesthood. He trained for that career in the Seminary of St. Sulpice and in the Sorbonne, becoming an abbé at nineteen and a prior of the Sorbonne when he was twenty-two.

But the priesthood could not satisfy his precocious mind. With his father's death in 1750, when Turgot was twenty-three, and his inheritance of adequate means of support, he abandoned his clerical career and began actively participating in political life.

He established a reputation as an effective and incorruptible official in the capacity of administrator of Limoges, with the title of Intendant, during the years 1761 to 1774. Recognition of both qualities by Louis XVI resulted in Turgot's appointment to the post of minister of marine. Shortly thereafter, with reform of the French economy in mind, Louis XVI, in one of his better exercises of judgment, transferred Turgot to the critical post of comptroller general of finance.

Turgot did a splendid job in that position. In the short period in which he served he almost accomplished the miracle of balancing the budget. Integrity and reformist zeal, however, did not appeal to a powerful group at court which included the queen, Marie Antoinette. Louis succumbed to pressure and Turgot resigned in 1776, less than two years after he assumed the office of comptroller general. Speculation suggests that had he continued in office and carried on his reforms, Louis XVI and Marie Antoinette might have escaped the guillotine.[1] With Turgot's resignation, the last, best chance for reform was lost.[2] For the remaining years of his life until his death in 1781 at the age of fifty-four, Turgot lived the quiet life of a retiree occupied with study.

The relevance to Condorcet of this brief recital of Turgot's political career is its relation to the influence Turgot had on Condorcet's life. One objective measure of that influence is the fact that when Turgot was appointed comptroller general, he named his friend, the Marquis de Condorcet, the inspector of the mint, and when Turgot resigned in 1776, Condorcet also resigned his position as inspector of the mint as soon as the Swiss banker, Jacques Necker, was appointed to take Turgot's place.

Senior to Condorcet by sixteen years, Turgot may have represented the father figure of which Condorcet was deprived by the death of his father when he was an infant. In a broad sense, Turgot's influence on Condorcet probably derived from the compatability of their minds and from Turgot's intellectual achievements, for Turgot was that interesting combination of the practical man of affairs who is also a stimulating thinker and writer, in short, a philosophe of the first rank.

His special field of intellectual interest was economic theory. In 1766 he wrote *Réflexions sur la formation et distribution des Richesse* (Reflections on the formation and distribution of riches), published serially in 1769 and 1770. It was an outline of economic theory, written for two Chinese students who were returning to China. The theory expounded in this treatise was that of the Physiocrats, the name of a school of eighteenth-century economic thought associated with two principal ideas: One idea, now outmoded, regarded land as the ultimate source of wealth and proposed a single tax payable only by landowners. The other idea, still very much alive, was their fervent advocacy of complete laisser faire or free trade and their opposition to mercantilism, the eighteenth-century word for protectionism.[3]

One of Turgot's accomplishments as comptroller general of finance was the removal of internal restraints and burdens on economic freedom. For example, he removed all governmental restrictions on the sale of grain within France.[4] He also abolished the infamous, if hallowed, relic of serfdom, the *corvée*, and the equally traditional, but extremely restrictive monopoly of the guilds. In the former the economic burden fell on those least able to sustain it—the peasants, who were required by the state or the lord of an estate to give a certain number of days, without compensation, to building and repairing roads. In the latter the opportunity of freely participating in the practice of a traditional craft was restricted to a favored few—the sons and sons-in-law of those who controlled the guilds.

While Condorcet was too independent in his thinking to blindly follow any formal school of thought, his underlying commitment to the idea of freedom made him a promoter of physiocratic doctrine, especially its espousal of free trade. Accordingly he was an enthusiastic supporter of Turgot's program and a passionate opponent of Turgot's successor, Jacques Necker, whose economic philosophy was the very antithesis of the physiocrats' in general and Turgot's in particular.

Because of their close friendship, the question of Turgot's

influence upon Condorcet's ideas is an interesting one. On that subject it should be said that friendship cannot be explained solely in terms of compatability of ideas. There is a chemistry of friendship that frequently defies strong differences of outlook and opinion. If the next census were to include a category of devout Democrats and equally devout Republicans who are friends, it assuredly would include large numbers of Americans whose friendships disregard differences in their political affiliations and inclinations. Of course a certain prescription for enduring friendship is a combination of the mysterious chemistry of friendship and agreement in principle upon points of view regarding matters of importance. The friendship between Turgot and Condorcet seems to have been founded on that happy combination of chemistry and ideas.

On one subject, economics, the probability is that Turgot was the leader and Condorcet was the follower, because that was Turgot's special field of interest and because he spent many years in practical experience as an administrator and, ultimately, as comptroller general of finance.

On other matters, however, the direction of their thinking was predictable, not because they influenced each other to think alike, but because both were philosophes in temperament, inclination, and outlook. By nature as well as by reason the perspective of each of them was humanitarian. Each possessed deeply felt social sensibilities, especially the yearning for universal freedom and for tolerance in human relations. Both were passionately committed to the need for reform. They were two strong-minded, independent, incorruptibly honest men whose points of view could not be changed or channeled in directions that did not satisfy their inner standards of rightness and probity. Each in his own, individual way was a philosophe by conviction and shared with the other philosophes a consensus of ideas regarding the power of reason and the necessity of change in political, religious, and educational philosophy and practice, all of which was embraced in the word Enlightenment. Their differences were not in the objectives they had charted for reform but in the development and expression of those ideas.

Notes

1. When Turgot took office as comptroller general the government's annual revenue was 213,500,000 francs, and its annual expenditures amounted to 235,000,000 francs. See Will and Ariel Durant, *Rousseau and Revolution,* vol. 10 of *The Story of Civilization* (New York: Simon and Schuster, 1967), p. 859.

2. Turgot is reported to have said to Louis at the time of his forced resignation, "Remember, sire, that it was weakness which brought the head of Charles I to the block."

3. Stated briefly in another way, the mercantile system considered "the goal of a state" to be "the accumulation of precious metals by exporting the largest possible quantity of its products and importing as little as possible, thus establishing a favorable balance of trade" (*Random House Dictionary of the English Language—The Unabridged Edition*).

4. Pursuant to an edict enacted on September 13, 1774, all governmental restrictions on the sale of grain within the realm were removed except in Paris.

15

"Condorcet, the Good"

Among his friends Condorcet was known not just as Condorcet but, affectionately and respectfully, as *Le Bon Condorcet*, "Condorcet, the Good." *Le Bon* was the accolade bestowed upon him by those who knew him best and were so impressed by his goodness that "Good" became an appropriate and inseparable part of his name. Julie de Lespinasse, the presiding genius of the brilliant salon at the rue de Belle Chasse and a superb judge of men, gave this warm appraisal of Condorcet's character:

> The appearance of M. de Condorcet announces the most distinctive and most absolute quality of his soul, its goodness. His physiognomy is sweet and calm; simplicity and negligence mark his bearing.[1]

The goodness of which Julie de Lespinasse so affectionately wrote was that of a man who by nature and inclination was not only good in his personal relationships but also in his passionate commitment to the promotion of justice and the welfare of human beings, individually and collectively in a broad social sense. Condorcet was good not in an abstract, philosophical way, remote from the affairs of everyday life. He was deeply involved in contemporary life, both at home and abroad. He was good in the sense of a warm and compassionate concern for his fellow human beings, individuals as well as the masses. His goodness encompassed all who suffered the indignity of injustice and oppression, whoever and wherever they might be.

Two examples will illustrate the depth of the humanitarian impulses that motivated him:

The first, an incident that occurred in 1786, involved three peasants who were accused of burglary. They were tried, convicted, and sentenced to being "broken on the wheel," a form of punishment designed to inflict torture. The evidence of guilt produced at the trial was not persuasive, and public sentiment was against this inhumane form of punishment. One unusual judge, named Dupaty, challenged the sentence and campaigned aggressively in favor of the condemned men. For his efforts in their behalf he was forced out of office by his associates.

Condorcet, outraged by the sentence and the ouster of Judge Dupaty, vigorously entered the fray by writing several pamphlets denouncing the court that had sentenced the accused men to suffer torture and forcefully supporting Judge Dupaty.[2] Condorcet's attack in this case contributed to a happy ending: a royal pardon of the accused men was granted and Judge Dupaty was restored to his office. The affair also resulted in a happy result for Condorcet. This will be the subject of the next chapter.

The second example relates to the international problem of slavery: Condorcet was instrumental in the organization of an antislavery society, called the *Société des amis des Noirs* (Society of the friends of the blacks). His associates in the formation of that organization included Lafayette and Mirabeau. Subsequently he became president of the society. In 1781 he published a pamphlet, entitled "Réflexions sur l'esclavage des Nègres (Reflections on Negro slavery), which was a logical and incisive condemnation of slavery on both humanitarian and economic grounds.

Subsequently, in the summer of 1788, the king announced that the Estates General, an almost forgotten institution, which allegedly represented the nation, would convene in the following spring. In the course of the election to that body, Condorcet appealed to the voters to demand the end of slavery in Santo Domingo, at that time a French possession. In 1789, when the National Assembly was organized, Condorcet appealed to that body to disqualify the representatives from Santo Domingo on the ground that their position as slave owners did not confer on them the right to represent their slaves.[3]

In August of that year, the National Assembly formulated the "Declaration of the Rights of Man," a bench mark of the French Revolution which incorporated the ideas of the philosophes. True to his unwavering opposition to slavery, Condorcet argued before the assembly that black people, like white people, are human beings and therefore are entitled to the same natural rights as white people. If slavery was not abolished, he insisted that the "Declaration of the Rights of Man" should be changed. He then proposed the adoption of a challenging and revealing limitation of the Declaration—that it should be modified to provide that "all white men are free and equal in rights, and give a rule on determining the degree of whiteness required."[4]

While that tongue-in-cheek proposal was not seriously considered, the point that it made may have helped to achieve the desired result. Despite its intemperate career, the National Convention (see chapter 21) did adopt social and political reforms, including the abolition, in 1794, of slavery in the French colonies.[5]

Notes

1. From Charles Henry, ed., *Lettres inédite de Mlle. de Lespinasse* (Paris, 1887). See Keith M. Baker, *Condorcet: From Natural Philosophy to Social Mathematics* (Chicago: University of Chicago Press, 1982), pp. 24, 403, and 501.

2. E. Seligman, *La justice en France pendant la Révolution* (Paris, 1913), vol. 1, pp. 99–102. See J. Salwyn Schapiro, *Condorcet and the Rise of Liberalism* (New York: Octagon Books, 1963), p. 75.

3. See Schapiro, *Condorcet and the Rise of Liberalism*, pp. 79 and 148.

4. Quoted by Alengry, *Condorcet*, 451. See Schapiro, *Condorcet and the Rise of Liberalism*, pp. 148 and 294.

5. John S. Garraty and Peter Gay, eds., *The Columbia History of the World* (New York: Harper and Row, 1987), p. 771; Schapiro, *Condorcet and the Rise of Liberalism*, p. 294.

16

The Ménage à Trois and Marriage

Gabrielle Émilie Le Tonnelier de Breteuil (1706–1749), daughter of the Baron de Breteuil, was married at the age of nineteen to Florent Claude, Marquis du Châtelet, then thirty. In due course she gave birth to three children. At that point in their lives, although they remained married, the Marquis and the Marquise appear to have lost interest in each other insofar as sex relations are concerned.

The Marquise had an extraordinary mind and an unusual education. She learned Latin, Italian, English, mathematics, and astronomy and not only understood Newtonian physics but translated the *Principia* into French. Voltaire was beguiled by the Marquise as an intellect as well as a woman. "How fortunate I am," he said, in his own unique style, that "I can admire her whom I love."[1]

Consequently, in about 1734, when she was twenty-eight and he was forty, the Marquise and Voltaire became lovers, with the knowledge, consent, and approval of the Marquis. For ten years, from 1734 to 1744, the Marquise, Voltaire, and, from time to time, the Marquis, resided together, in the Marquis's ancestral home located at Cirey, a village in northeastern France, near Lorraine.

This excursion into the ménage à trois of Voltaire and the du Châtelets is made to point up the fact that in the circles in which they traveled it was a socially acceptable relationship. At that time, in that place, and in that milieu, utility, rather than love, was generally the compelling factor in the arrangement or making of marriages. Insofar as the royal family and the nobility were concerned, marriage was considered to be a matter of convenience, serving political and economic considerations rather than love.

In the case of the king the primary purpose of the bond of marriage was largely the achievement of a political objective. When Louis XIV died in 1715, his successor, his great grandson, Louis XV, was just five years old. Philippe II, Duc d'Orléans, a nephew of Louis XIV, thereupon became regent, in effect the ruler of France during the minority of Louis. For reasons of state the young king at age eleven in 1721 was officially betrothed to the Spanish Infanta, then all of age two. When Louis was thirteen, however, Philippe died and the regency was placed in the hands of the Duc de Bourbon.

His vision of the future of Louis XV was different from that of Philippe. When the king, during the regency of the Duc de Bourbon, celebrated his fifteenth birthday in 1725, the Infanta was only five. Confronted by the undeniable fact that she could not be expected to bear an heir to the throne for some years, the Duc de Bourbon, as regent, decided, unilaterally, to terminate the king's betrothal to the Infanta and thereupon arranged the marriage of Louis XV, at age fifteen, to Marie Leczinska, daughter of Stanislas, the former king of Poland. She was "six years older than Louis XV and no beauty," but, on the other hand, "she was healthy and seemed capable of guaranteeing the succession."[2]

Obviously this was an arrangement of convenience in which Louis XV was a pawn rather than a chooser. When Louis was sufficiently the master of his life and had the freedom of choice, he selected as his mistress Jeanne Antoine Poisson, subsequently known as the Marquise de Pompadour. She was eleven years his junior, a woman of great beauty, wit, and a first-rate mind.[3]

In the case of the nobility marriage was frequently a useful method for the acquisition of economic benefits. Financially insecure members of the nobility repaired their fortunes through marriage to affluent representatives of the bourgeoisie, using titles as the equivalent consideration for financial security.

Quite likely that was the case in the marriage of Condorcet's parents. His father, the poor but noble Antoine, was the captain of a cavalry regiment stationed in a garrison at Ribemont in Picardy. There he met and married Condorcet's mother, Marie-Madeleine-Catherine de Saint Felix, a young bourgeois widow who happened to be attractively wealthy.

The members of the well-to-do bourgeoisie also subordinated the premise of love in marriage to issues of utility such as financial security and the attraction of social advancement. Mme. Geoffrin, one of the great *salonnières* of eighteenth-century France, upon the advice of her grandmother with whom she lived, was married at the age of thirteen to François Geoffrin, who was then forty-eight but wealthy. The motivation was assuredly not love on the part of the thirteen-year-old bride but her obedient acquiescence to her grandmother's desire to assure the security of her granddaughter's future.

Thus, whereas the twentieth-century remedy in the United States for the absence of love in marriage is divorce, the eighteenth-century French prescription for the same problem was not divorce but adultery. It was openly practiced and socially approved through the creation of an arrangement in which the consenting parties were known as lover and mistress, an arrangement given the ultimate seal of social approval by the example of the king. In an age when marriages were formed for economic benefits and social prestige and power, the mores accommodated natural sexual urges through the arrangement of lover and mistress.

To that rule the Marquis de Condorcet was an exception and an anomaly. He had no mistress. At a time of license, he was a puritan who married for love and, remarkable to relate, did not request or receive a dowry from the wealthy father of the bride.

The woman who became his wife was Sophie de Grouchy, the niece of Judge Dupaty, whom Condorcet would not have met but for his work on behalf of her uncle. She was the daughter of the Marquis de Grouchy and was young, beautiful, and intelligent. They fell in love and were married in 1786 when Condorcet was forty-three and his bride twenty-two.

The marriage was a happy one, partly because they shared the same intellectual interests and sympathies. Both, for example, knew English, and she was so accomplished that she translated into French Adam Smith's *Theory of Moral Sentiments* and Thomas Paine's speeches to the National Assembly. Under her guidance their home became one of the great salons of Paris, frequented not only by the outstanding French intellectuals but by Americans as well, including Jefferson and Paine. They had one child, Alexandrine-Louise-Sophie, born in 1790, who married General O'Connor, an Irish refugee who served under Napoleon.

Unfortunately, because of Condorcet's flight from persecution and his untimely death, his happy marriage to Sophie lasted only eight years. She remained a widow until her death in 1823. The intervening years, however, were productive. Because of her devotion to Condorcet, posterity is indebted to her for the first complete edition of his work, entitled *Oeuvres complète de Condorcet*, published in twenty-one volumes in Paris in 1804.[4]

Fourteen years before meeting Sophie de Grouchy, Condorcet had formed one other significant relationship with a woman named Amélie Suard and her husband, Jean Baptists Antoine Suard, a journalist. This friendship would later prove to be his undoing. They were among the personalities who frequented the salon of Julie de Lespinasse. In a sense, Condorcet became involved in a ménage à trois, although his part in it appears to have been platonic. The Suard's friendship with Condorcet ripened, and for two years, from 1772 to 1774, he lived in their home.

At the time he was in love with a Mme. De Meulon, but his love was not reciprocated by her. Rather than playing the role of mistress, Amélie Suard was his confidant, adviser, and, perhaps, his therapist, regarding his unrequited passion.

Condorcet's residence in the Suard home ended in 1774, when Turgot, as comptroller general of finance, appointed his friend Condorcet to the position of inspector of the mint (*inspecteur des monnaies*). Thereupon Condorcet established his home in the Hotel des monnaies, one of the perquisites of that position. The Suards and Condorcet continued their friendship, but on a less intimate basis, for many years.

The link between them weakened, quite likely without Condorcet being aware of it, when he married Sophie de Grouchy, an event that aroused jealousy and stimulated a bit of malice on the part of Amélie who characterized Sophie as an "intriguing, and ambitious woman."[5] The breaking point in the relationship, insofar as the Suards were concerned, stemmed from their disapproval of the part Condorcet played during the Revolution.

At the end of his life, when Condorcet left his hiding place in the pension of Mme. Vernet, in order to protect her, he headed for sanctuary in the home of his old friends, apparently unaware of the change in their feelings for him. But the Suards refused to help him and turned him away. One can only imagine his despair, a fugitive from death, left to wander aimlessly, without shelter or food until arrest, imprisonment, and death caught up with him in Bourg-La-Reims in March 1794.

Notes

1. Will and Ariel Durant, *The Age of Voltaire*, vol. 9 of *The Story of Civilization* (New York: Simon and Schuster, 1965), p. 366.

2. Alfred Cobban, *A History of Modern France*, vol. 1: 1715–1799 (New York: Penguin, 1961), p. 28.

3. Through her acknowleged position as the king's mistress, she acquired and exercised both influence and authority, frequently in unexpected directions. She was admired, in fact by the philosophes. Through her position she was helpful to Voltaire, Diderot, and the continued publication of the *Encyclopédie*.

4. Sophie was assisted in the preparation of this edition by A. A. Barbier, P. J. G. Cabanis, and D. J. Garat. Subsequently a second edition of Condorcet's work was edited by Condorcet's daughter and François Arago, entitled *Oeuvres de Condorcet*, published in twelve volumes in Paris (1847–1849).

5. Keith M. Baker, *Condorcet: From Natural Philosophy to Social Mathematics* (Chicago: University of Chicago Press, 1982), p. 26.

17

The Oeuvres of Condorcet

Although the young Marquis de Condorcet arrived in Paris from Ribemont intent upon embarking on the career of mathematician and scientist, the influences of life in Paris changed the direction of his life. While his interest in mathematics and science was not abandoned, it was subordinated to that of a writer and an activist in the support and advocacy of causes for the betterment of the human condition.

When the twenty-one volumes of the first edition of his collected writings were published, some were mathematical, scientific, biographical, and philosophical, but most dealt with causes—social, economic, and political. They were written in the form of letters, essays, pamphlets, articles, and books, all fueled by a consuming desire to do "good" and a passion to improve the lives of people, a desire once expressed by him in a letter to Turgot written in 1772, in which he said, "You are very fortunate to combine the passion for the public good with the position to achieve it."[1] In time he, too, was able to combine both the passion to do good and the position to achieve it.

It is interesting to trace the circumstances that produced the change in the direction of Condorcet's career. D'Alembert, his mentor, it will be recalled, conducted a campaign to have his protégé elected as secretary of the Academy of Sciences. That project required a bit of intrigue involving the incumbent secretary, the elderly Grandjean de Fouchy, who was contemplating retirement. His support for Condorcet as a successor was considered to be important.

It had long been the practice of the secretary to write *éloges* about members of the Academy at the time of their death. One of the prerequisites for election to the position of secretary, therefore, was the ability to write an acceptable biography. Accordingly, Julie de Lespinasse advised Condorcet "to write a few pieces."[2] Following that suggestion, Condorcet wrote a biographical essay about Fontaine, a deceased mathematician, and sent it to Mlle. de Lespinasse. She, in turn, delivered it to d'Alembert. He used it to demonstrate Condorcet's ability to write and succeeded in persuading Grandjean de Fouchy to give Condorcet the assignment of writing the official *éloge* of Fontaine.

Winning the approval of the incumbent secretary was only the first step in the campaign to elect Condorcet as his successor. It was then necessary to persuade the members of the Academy that he had the requisite writing ability. For that purpose Condorcet conceived the idea of writing a collection of eleven biographies of academicians who had died during the period of thirty-three years from the founding of the Academy in 1666 to 1699 when the practice of writing *éloges* had begun. This effort was greeted with rapturous approval by Condorcet's friends, perhaps exaggerated in the interest of electing their favorite son.

In any event, the campaign for the election of Condorcet was successful. He was elected assistant secretary of the Academy in 1773 at the age of thirty and was thereby launched on the career of being a man of letters and a philosophe in the service of the common good.[3]

Equipped with his newly discovered ability to write and immersed in the company that frequented the salon of Julie de Lespinasse, it is understandable, without attempting to psycho-analyze Condorcet, that the direction of his thinking and his interests underwent a change. Perhaps, too, the change in direction was stimulated by his meeting with Voltaire in 1770 when, it will be recalled, Julie de Lespinasse fortuitously drafted Condorcet to accompany d'Alembert on a mission to regain his health at Ferney. That visit created a lasting friendship between Voltaire and Condorcet and probably contributed materially to Condorcet's name being known to history as a philosophe rather than as a mathematician.

The first notable sign of that change in direction occurred in 1773 in an anonymous and angry letter written by Condorcet, entitled "Letter of a Theologian to the Author of the *Dictionary of Three Centuries.*"[4] The impetus for the writing of the letter was a book by the abbé Antoine Sabatier entitled *Three Centuries of Our Literature,*[5] in which he attacked the *Encyclopédie* and the philosophes who supported and contributed to it as "a monstrous cabal with a subversive stranglehold on French letters." To that charge Sabatier added a denunciation of the philosophes as "the natural enemies of the princes."[6]

Condorcet viewed Sabatier's attack as not only intellectual but personal, since his friend d'Alembert was a co-editor of the *Encyclopédie* with Diderot. It was an attack that Condorcet could not ignore. Vehemently he defended "the party of humanity from the calumnies of fanaticism."[7] The aristocrat by birth, but the democrat by choice, sharply responded to Sabatier: "While you by conscious choice permit kings to oppress people . . . the philosophes have made known to the kings the cries of the people and have not been afraid to speak to them of their rights."

From that point on to the end of his life, the mind and pen of Condorcet was engaged in defending human rights.

The underlying objective that motivated him was the desire to achieve reform—economic, political, and social—in France and elsewhere. The underlying premises that infused his concepts of reform were the application to the human condition of the ideas of freedom, reason, tolerance, and justice.

So it was that in the succeeding years Condorcet, brimming with ideas for improvement, advocated free trade, freedom of speech, freedom of press, the end of censorship, the end of slavery, the enfranchisement of women, universal free education, equality before the law, the separation of state and church, religious toleration, the adoption of a written constitution with a written declaration of the rights of people embedded in the constitution to insure the recognition of those rights, the establishment of a representative or parliamentary form of national government, and local self-government to encourage the independence and the participation of the peasants in government.[8] Added to this output were his contributions to the Encyclopédie, his biographies of Voltaire and Turgot, his éloges of academicians who died during his term of office, a kind of continuing history of science in eighteenth-century France, two essays on the intriguing subject of probabilities and, at the very end, his contribution to posterity of the prophetic, optimistic Sketch.

There is an interesting connecting link between Condorcet's essays dealing with the subject of probabilities, written before the French Revolution, and his final work, the Sketch, written while he was in hiding, a victim of the French Revolution. Newton and Locke had bequeathed as their legacy strong arguments for the power of reason and its ability to reveal the laws that govern the operations of the universe. Condorcet was persuaded that if reason can determine the laws that govern the physical world, it can also determine, albeit with less exactitude, the laws that govern mankind's social relations. To that end he developed in two essays a theory of probability applicable to the social sciences. Fundamentally a mathematician at heart, he was intrigued by the idea of applying the calculus of probabilities as the tool for the achievement of that objective.

In the unfinished "General View of Science That Has For Its Objective the Application of Calculus to the Moral and Political Sciences" (*Tableau générale de la science, qui a pour objet l'application du calcul aux sciences morale et politique*) Condorcet sought to establish that the calculus of probabilities is as applicable to the science of man as it is to the physical sciences. In his "Essay on the Application of Analysis to the Probability of Majority Decisions" (*Essai sur l'application de l'analyze à la probabilité des décisions rendues à la pluralité des voix*) his objective was to discover by means of the calculus of probabilities the conditions under which there will be an adequate guarantee that the majority decision of an assembly is true. Implicit in his concept of probability is the idea of predictability. That is the premise of the *Sketch*—that based on a review of the history of human development, one can, with reason, predict the future course of the human story.

With these words of passionate conviction he opened his case for that proposition in the tenth chapter of the *Sketch:*

If man can, with almost complete assurance, predict phenomena when he knows their laws, and if, even when he does not, he can still, with great expectation of success, forecast the future on the basis of his experience of the past, why, then, should it be regarded as a fantastic undertaking to sketch, with some pretense to truth, the future destiny of man on the basis of his history? The sole foundation for belief in the natural sciences is this idea, that the general laws directing the phenomena of the universe, known or unknown, are necessary and constant. Why should this principle be any less true for the development of the intellectual or moral faculties of man than for the other operations of nature?[9]

On that note he submitted for posterity his thoughts about progress at a time and in a world he envisioned, but would never see.[10]

Notes

1. Keith M. Baker, *Condorcet: From Natural Philosophy to Social Mathematics* (Chicago: University of Chicago Press, 1982), p. 26.
2. Ibid.
3. Condorcet was elected permanent secretary on August 7, 1776.
4. *Lettres d'un theologien à l'auteur du Dictionnaire des trois siècles.*
5. *Trois siécles de notre litérature.*
6. Baker, *Condorcet*, p. 34.
7. Ibid., p. 34.
8. Some of these ideas were expressed in such writings as *Lettres d'un bourgeois de New Haven* (a pamphlet of imaginary letters from a person living in New Haven); *Essai sur la constitution et les fonctions des assemblées provinciale* (Essay on the constitution and the functions of provincial assemblies); *Lettres d'un citoyen des Etats-Unis* (Letters of a citizen of the United States); *Idées sur le despotisme* (Ideas about despotism); and *Declaration des droits* (Declaration of rights).
   Condorcet advocated a unicameral legislature. He was so strongly committed to the protection of the rights of people that he opposed giving the courts the right to interpret the law. Instead he proposed

the Right of Censure (*Droit de Censure*), a popular veto of the national legislature, and provision for the amendment of the constitution periodically by conventions every twenty years.

9. *Sketch for a Historical Picture of the Progress of the Human Mind,* trans. June Barraclough (New York: Noonday Press, 1955; reprint—Hyperion Press, 1979), p. 173.

10. Other aspects of the work of Condorcet are discussed in the context of the following chapters.

Part Four

Condorcet and the French Revolution

18

Introduction

The years 1789 to 1793 were the years when Condorcet participated in the French Revolution as the last remaining philosophe. After a lifetime of preparation, those four years presented to him the opportunity of realizing the aspirations and concepts of the Enlightenment through his writing, speeches, and proposals for constitutional reform.

Three assemblies of representatives were convened in Paris to consider and act upon the reform of the government of France. They were, in the order of their service, the National Assembly, the Legislative Assembly, and the National Convention. Condorcet was a member of the latter two but not the former. However, officially and unofficially, as hereafter noted, he exercised, as a constant protagonist of the agenda of the philosophes for reform, an important influence upon the National Assembly's deliberations and decisions.

Because of his involvement in the work of the various revolutionary assemblies that convened between 1789 and 1793, clarity requires the review, in some measure, of the history of those assemblies in order to appraise Condorcet's role in the French Revolution.

19

The National Assembly

The first and most significant of these assemblies was the National Assembly, which convened for the first time on June 17, 1789. Its establishment was in and of itself a revolutionary event. June 17, 1789, can be considered the beginning of the revolution, although the French celebrate July 14, 1789, the date of the storming of the Bastille, as their Independence Day.

The National Assembly that met for the first time on June 17, 1789, was an offshoot of the Estates General, a French institution which supposedly represented the nation but had not convened in the preceding 175 years.[1] The Estates General consisted of three "Estates." The clergy was the First Estate; the nobility the Second; and the commoners—peasants, urban workers, and the bourgeoisie—the Third.

The immediate circumstance that motivated the king's order directing the convening of the Estates General for the first time since 1614 was the severe financial crisis confronting the nation and his inability through his ministers to persuade the members of the First and Second Estates to contribute to the solution of

171

the problem of rescuing France from bankruptcy. The comptroller general of finances had convened the Assembly of Notables, consisting of the principal members of the clergy and the nobles, for the purpose of presenting the crisis to them and impressing them with both its severity and the necessity of their help by bearing a larger share of the burden of taxation. When the Assembly of Notables rejected that proposal, Louis XVI conceded, in effect, his inability to deal with the situation and, in desperation, he dissolved the Assembly of Notables and called upon an institution that the monarchy had for so long ignored as the vehicle of last resort. It was then that the Third Estate asserted itself.

The precedent of the past was that each Estate deliberated separately and that the passage of a measure required the consent of two estates and the approval of the king. In 1789 the Third Estate insisted upon and obtained double representation, thereby acquiring as many seats as the clergy and nobility combined, and then demanded "voting by head" instead of "voting by order." The impasse created by that demand resulted in a decision by the Third Estate on June 17, 1789, to strike out on its own by proclaiming itself to be the National Assembly and inviting the deputies of the two other estates to join it.[2] Some of them did, mainly members of the clergy of low rank in the pecking order. Ten days later, after some vacillation, the king ordered the members of the First and Second Estates to join the National Assembly. That was the end of the Estates General and confirmation that a revolution was in progress.[3]

Three days after the declaration of independence of the Third Estate on June 17, 1789, the newly created National Assembly set the revolution in motion by resolving never to disband until it had adopted a new constitution for France. In its brief existence of a little more than two years, between June 1789 and October

1791, the National Assembly changed the government of France from an absolute monarchy to a constitutional monarchy. It abolished feudalism, including the last vestiges of serfdom. It also abolished torture as a method of punishment, the practices of arbitrary arrest and imprisonment, and persecution for heresy.[4] It recognized as political rights freedom of opinion in matters of religion and freedom from taxation without consent. In the retrospect of history, it achieved what is probably its most memorable accomplishment—the adoption of the Declaration of the Rights of Man and Citizen, echoing the ideas of the philosophes.

The Declaration asserted in Article I, "Men are born free and equal in rights," and in Article II it defined those rights, stating, "These rights are liberty, property, security and resistance to oppression." Liberty was accorded a definition in Article IV, which stated that it is "the exercise of the natural rights of each man" circumscribed only by the "limits determined by law." "Law" was also a term whose definition was not left to chance. Article VI stated, "Law is the expression of the general will" and, further, that "all citizens have the right to take part, in person or by their representatives in its formation." On the fundamental subject of the guarantee of rights, Article XVI stated, "Any society in which the guarantee of rights is not assured or the separation of powers not determined has no constitution."

This was the philosophy of Enlightenment incorporated into the political and legal structure of France by an effective legislative body representing the majority of its people. Condorcet, by the circumstance of his birth in 1743, was the fortunate one among the philosophes to live long enough to witness, on August 26, 1789, at the age of forty-six, the transformation of theory about the rights of mankind into the reality of recognition and guarantee by the Declaration.[5]

True to its prescription concerning rights the National Assembly, after nearly two years of discussion, adopted a constitution in the summer of 1791, incorporating many of the ideas of the Enlightenment. Among these was the principle of the separation of powers. The constitution of 1789 provided for the division of power among an elected single legislative chamber, elected judges, and the king as the executive head of the government, who was reduced in status from an absolute monarch by divine right to a constitutionally created king with limited powers.[6] Significantly, in this connection, the king's title was changed by decree from "Louis, by grace of God, King of France and Navarre" to "Louis, by the grace of God and the constitutional law of the state, King of the French." To emphasize the shift in the source of authority in France, the Declaration of Rights said, "The source of all sovereignty resides essentially in the nation."

Other changes, indicative of the broadly based feeling of displeasure with the church and the clergy, was the National Assembly's adoption of a series of measures designed to curb their power and to subject them to civil control. Church lands were nationalized in 1789 and some of them were sold as the means of solving the financial crisis on the premise that "the wealth of the clergy is at the disposition of the nation." In 1790 the religious orders were suppressed. In the same year the National Assembly adopted the Civil Constitution of the Clergy, requiring the clergy to take an oath of loyalty to "be faithful to the nation, to the law, and to the King and to maintain with all their power the Constitution decreed by the National Assembly and accepted by the King." The National Assembly also decreed that bishops and priests should be elected, that marriage was a civil contract, and that public education should be both free and secular.[7]

One practical nonideological accomplishment of the National Assembly, which has left a permanent imprint on France, was the creation of an orderly, logical pattern of administrative divisions and subdivisions similar to our states, counties, and municipalities, except that they were called departments, districts (*arrondissements*), and communes.[8] They replaced a patchwork of disorderly, illogical divisions, which in the course of time had accrued haphazardly.

In at least one respect, sound judgment yielded to bitter resentment against the church and the clergy by the enactment of the constitutional provisions changing the status of bishops and priests (non-Catholic as well as Catholic) to that of civil officials, who were paid by the state and elected by the people. That created a serious conflict with the authority of the pope, alienated many devout Catholics, and furnished a strong cause for opposition to the revolution.

Disturbances broke out in rural areas and, beginning in the summer of 1789, large numbers of the nobility and clergy fled from France to Germany. There they gathered for the purpose of engaging Austrian and Russian support for a counterrevolution.

Two years later the king made the fatal mistake of trying to join the *emigres*, with the idea of obtaining foreign aid to restore his authority. He and Marie Antoinette fled on June 20, 1791, disguised as a valet and a governess. On the following day they were recognized at Varennes in Northeastern France and were brought back to the Tuileries in Paris, where their status, in effect, was that of humiliated and carefully guarded prisoners. Louis XVI, undoubtedly reluctantly and apprehensively, affixed his signature to the new constitution on Septembar 14, 1791.

Sixteen days later, on September 30, 1791, the career of the National Assembly ended. That Assembly, in an act of self-abnegation maneuvered by Robespierre, adopted an ordinance disqualifying its members from participating in its successor. This act of self-denial, motivated by the desire of high-minded, moderate men to avoid the stigma of promoting self-interest, had the unfortunate effect of diminishing moderation and insuring the danger of extremism in the character of its successor.[9] The Legislative Assembly, successor to the National Assembly, convened for the first time on October 1, 1791. Its career was relatively brief, ending less than a year later on September 20, 1792.

Condorcet, as previously noted, served as a member of both the "Legislative Assembly" and its successor, the "Convention," but not as a member of the National Assembly, their predecessor. He sought election to the National Assembly but was rejected by his own "Estate," the nobility, probably because he was too liberal for their taste. When the king had issued his call for the convening of the Estates General for the first time in 175 years, Condorcet opposed the call precisely because the Estates General was controlled by the privileged classes. Insisting that control by nobles and clergy, who represented a minority of the population, was a violation of natural rights, he demanded that the members of an assembly representing the nation should be elected by popular vote. He urged the Assembly of the nobility to join the Estates of the clergy and the commoners in a single assembly, which voted by head instead of by class. Undoubtedly that appeal was the reason for his not being elected to the Assembly.

Nevertheless, while not a member of the National Assembly, he occupied several strategic positions during its tenure, which secured for him the hearing and the consideration of his views. He served as a member of the municipal government of Paris, as a founding member of the Society of 1789, as an editor of and a contributor to the *Journal of the Society of 1789*, as a founder and editor of another journal, *La Republicaine*, as the chairman of a commission of the treasury, and as a prestigious member of the French Academy. In each of these capacities he was a constant, persistent exponent and propagandist for democratic reform.

To put his career in perspective in relation to the National Assembly, time and place are important. Condorcet, the philosophe, was also a confirmed Parisian, by choice if not by birth, and Paris was the focal point of the Revolution, exercising a dominating influence upon its direction from beginning to end, commencing with the organization of the National Assembly on June 17, 1789, and the assault upon the Bastille less than a month later.

The municipal government of Paris, itself a creation of the revolution,[10] was at the center of this maelstrom. It was a focal point of pressure upon the National Assembly, demanding attention and consideration of its ideas. In addition the Assembly leaned heavily upon the municipal government for its security. To that authority Condorcet was elected, representing the St. Germain district.

The prevention of anarchy and the restoration of order after the storming of the Bastille was the first order of business to which Condorcet addressed himself as a member of the revolutionary municipal government. He was a member of a delegation that met with the king to discuss arrangements for maintaining quiet and stability in Paris. He prompted the municipal government to send an address to the National Assembly, guaranteeing the safety of its members and the protection of its deliberations from interference. He participated in the preparation of an address to the people of Paris, stressing the importance of an atmosphere of calmness for the achievement of the goals of the Revolution.

Then Condorcet directed his attention to the objectives of the Revolution, urging that anarchy could be avoided only by a Declaration of Rights and the adoption of a constitution assuring a representative government. The idea for a Declaration of Rights by the National Assembly had already been proposed by Condorcet as the foundation for constitutional reform when the king issued the call for the assembly of the Estates General.[11] Later, in his official capacity as a member of the municipal government of Paris, he pursued that idea by drafting a model for a Declaration of Rights, which he urged the National Assembly to adopt. The Declaration of the Rights of Man and Citizens, which the National Assembly did adopt, substantially follows the Condorcet draft, omitting, however, some of its more progressive features.[12]

As a member of the municipal government of Paris he also exercised the prerogative of a friend to criticize deviations by the National Assembly from the democratic ideal. For example, he campaigned in the municipal assembly against the National Assembly's adoption of property qualifications for voting and, especially, against similar qualifications for election to the legislature.[13]

Besides exercising influence upon the National Assembly in his capacity as a member of the municipal government, Condorcet also occupied the influential position of a founder and member of the Society of 1789, whose principal organizers were Condorcet and Abbé Sieyès. Early members were Lafayette and the duc de la Rochefoucauld, political friends of Condorcet. Other members were scientists, men of letters, financiers, and about one hundred deputies of the National Assembly not resident in Paris, who were accepted as associates of the Society. Ultimately, at the peak of its career, the Society had 413 members, providing an influential forum for the expression of ideas.

The Society's objectives were both scholarly and practical. It sought, on the one hand, to study the subject of government as a social science or "social art"[14] and then to apply the principles derived from that study to the practical business of the constitutional government of France. In carrying out those purposes the Society also published the *Journal of the Society of 1789*, of which Condorcet was the editor and a principal contributor of articles. From the vantage point of both positions, Condorcet made many contributions.

The Society was essentially a forum for the expression of liberal opinion supporting the idea of constitutional monarchy as the appropriate form of government for France. The flight of the king in June 1791 produced a split in the thinking of the members of the Society on that subject. Condorcet was one of those converted from support of a constitutional monarchy to advocacy of a republican form of government. In July 1791, one month after the king's attempt to escape, Condorcet delivered a powerful and, at that time, sensational speech, in support of a republican form of government. He denounced the king for trying to run away from France. He argued that in so doing, he had abdicated his throne and "was now as free of us as we are free of him."[15] "It was an event," said the premier French historian of the Revolution, "to hear the greatest thinker of that day . . . preach the republic."[16]

While, in the main, he supported the work of the National Assembly, his critical reaction to the disposition of four issues during the tenure of the National Assembly illustrates the quality of his mind and character:

Condorcet was a forceful advocate of the complete separation of church and state, and the secularization of education. Nevertheless he condemned the seizure of church property without compensation. Similarly, he criticized the National Assembly for its failure to provide pensions for the nuns and monks whose support by the religious orders had been terminated by the suppression of those orders.[17]

Condorcet, as previously noted, had faulted the National Assembly for its adoption of property qualifications for both voting and election to the legislature. In addition he took issue with the National Assembly for its failure to grant to women the right to vote. Notably far in advance of his time, he wrote a pamphlet in 1790, seeking to influence the National Assembly, entitled "On the Admission of Women to the Right of Suffrage,"[18] arguing that it was inequitable to deprive one half of humanity of the same political rights that were allotted to the other half.[19] On this issue, he was ahead not only of eighteenth-century but of nineteenth-century and early twentieth-century thought and action as well.

Even that brave, new democracy across the sea had not provided for the exercise of political rights by the "other half" of its citizens. In 1776 Abigail Adams, bright and forthright, had sent a letter to her husband while he was serving in the Continental Congress, expressing her outrage at the continued treatment of women as inferiors. Bluntly, she said, "That your sex are naturally tyrannical is a truth so thoroughly established as to admit of no dispute." Despite the fact that her husband John was the second president of the United States and her son John Quincy was the sixth president of the United States, the reform for which Abigail hoped did not arrive until almost 150 years after she charged her husband with knowledge of the tyranny of his sex.[20] Had the Marquis de Condorcet been the second or the sixth president of the United States it is highly probable, in view of his record, that he would have initiated and promoted the grant of voting rights to women, without prompting by Abigail Adams.

There is also a reasonable probability that the Marquis, an abolitionist at heart, would have proposed, if president, a program for the termination of slavery in the United States. It will be recalled from the preceding chapter that as a writer and in his capacity as president of the Society of the Friends of the Blacks, he importuned the voters and the National Assembly to end slavery in Santo Domingo and to disqualify the representatives of Santo Domingo, on the ground that they had no right to represent their slaves. He also demanded revision of the Declaration of the Rights of Man and Citizens to include the entitlement of blacks as well as whites to "natural rights."

Another area of critical dissent is revealed in his friendship and association with Tom Paine. Paine, the son of a Quaker corset maker, was born in England in 1737. In 1774, at the age of thirty-seven, just two years before the beginning of the American Revolution, he migrated to America. Despite his brief residence here, he quickly became famous for his contributions to the literature of the Revolution. Among these were *Common Sense,* produced in 1776, and a series of pamphlets collectively called the *Crisis,* written between 1776 and 1782.

It was in the *Crisis* paper of January 1777 that he wrote these stirring words:

> These are the times that try men's souls. The summer soldier and the sunshine patriot will, in this crisis, shrink from the service of their country; but he that stands it now deserves the love and thanks of man and woman. Tyranny, like hell, is not easily conquered. Yet we have this consolation with us, that the harder the conflict, the more glorious the triumph.

In 1787 Paine returned to England where he wrote *The Rights of Man* in 1791 and 1792. That work was a defense of the French Revolution in reply to Edmund Burke's critical *Reflection on the Revolution in France.* His attack on English institutions in several passages in *The Rights of Man* led to his prosecution for treason and his flight to France. There, this unusual man was made an honorary citizen in 1792 and also became a delegate to the National Convention, the assemblage that followed the National Assembly and the Legislative Assembly. The point of this excursion into the life of Thomas Paine is that despite the disparate backgrounds of Condorcet and Paine, the two men became friends and collaborators in the founding of a new journal called Le Républicain, edited by Condorcet.[21] (This alliance between Condorcet and Tom Paine also marked the end of Condorcet's friendship with Lafayette and the duc de la Rochefoucauld.)

Condorcet's actions and writings at the beginning of the Revolution demonstrate a mind governed by a sense of equity and character and marked by the qualities of humaneness and kindness. His position regarding slavery, the taking of church property without compensation, and the failure to provide pensions for the nuns and monks of suppressed orders all underscore these qualities. His position on the subject of women's rights reveals a progressive mind with a vision of the future far in advance of his time. Finally his advocacy of a republican form of government in spite of his aristocratic background and associations indicate a character controlled by reason and logic, consistent and constant in pursuing the logic of principle and possessing the toughness to do so even at the cost of friendship. In this respect Condorcet presents a casebook example of a rational, logical mind suppressing or shedding the powerful influences of biases, prejudices, and inherited opinion acquired during the malleable periods of childhood and adolescence. Such brilliance and morality transformed a member of the nobility into a committed republican as well as a democrat.

These credentials as a thinker, a man of integrity, and a republican were recognized by Condorcet's contemporaries. His intellectual and moral authority earned for him the title of "the first magistrate of reason in Europe."[22] The home of the aristocrat who had become a republican became known as the "foyer de la République," and the salon of the Condorcets was renamed "the natural center of thinking Europe."[23] When he was elected as a member of the Legislative Assembly his prestige was such that he was made successively one of its secretaries, then its vice president and, thereafter, its president.[24] And when, later, he sought election to the National Convention he had achieved such distinguished status that five districts vied for the honor of designating him as their representative.[25]

Notes

1. The National Assembly is sometimes referred to as the "Constituent Assembly." See, for example, Alfred Cobban, *A History of Modern France,* vol. 1: 1715–1799 (New York: Penguin Books, 1961), p. 163.

2. In so doing the Third Estate adopted the proposal that had been advanced by the Abbé Siéyès in his influential pamphlet, "*Qu'est-ce Que le Tier Etat?*" (What is the Third Estate?).

3. Alfred Cobban states: "Only when royal authority had been weakened and the king humiliated and forced to refer the problem of governing France to an elected assembly, did the Third Estate enter into the struggle in its own right, put forward its own claims, and in so doing transformed what had been an aristocratic Fronde into a revolution of a new kind, such as Europe had not witnessed before." (Cobban, *A History of Modern France,* vol. 1, p. 138.)

4. In August 1789, the Assembly adopted a series of "Decrees Abolishing the Feudal System," the opening words of which were "The National Assembly abolishes the feudal regime entirely."

5. See, however, *A History of Modern France,* vol. 1: 1715–1799, where Alfred Cobban takes the position that neither Rousseau's *Social Contract* "nor the writings of the philosophes" influenced the Declaration of Rights and that the sources "will be found in the Remonstrances of the Parlements, and behind these in the ideas of the Natural Law school of thought." (pp. 163–64).

6. The king was given veto power limited to four years.

7. It should also be noted that a more conservative measure was the adoption of a property qualification for voting, namely the payment of a tax "equivalent to the value of three days labor in the year." (Alfred Cobban, *A History of Modern France*, p. 167.)

8. Initially there were eighty-three departments which were approximately equal in size.

9. See Cobban, *A History of Modern France*, vol. 1: 1715–1799, p. 184.

10. The storming of the Bastille had also terminated the existing municipal government. "The electors, who had been chosen in the first place as secondary electors for Paris to the States-General but had never dissolved, now constituted themselves the municipal authority . . . and took over such government as the city was capable of." (Cobban, *A History of Modern France*, vol. 1: 1715–1799.)

11. See Keith Baker, *Condorcet: From Natural Philosophy to Social Mathematics* (Chicago: University of Chicago Press, 1982), p. 265, where it is said: "In the cahier of the nobility of Mantes that was largely his work, Condorcet stressed the need for a declaration of the rights of men and citizens as the foundation for constitutional reform outlining the principal articles that such a declaration would contain and emphasizing the importance of making its adoption the first essential order of business for the Estates-General."

12. Namely, the abolition of capital punishment, equality of inheritance by children regardless of differences in age or sex, and the preservation of natural rights during times of war as well as peace. See J. Salwyn Schapiro, *Condorcet and the Rise of Liberalism* (New York: Octagon Books, 1963), p. 84.

13. See Baker, *Condorcet*, p. 268.

14. "As its purpose was defined in Sieyès's pamphlet and elaborated by Condorcet in the prospectus for its journal, the enlarged Society of 1789 was to have two closely related aims: the development of 'the social art' and the application of its principles to the establishment of a new constitution." (Baker, *Condorcet*, p. 273.)

15. F. Buisson, ed., *Condorcet*, p. 45. See Schapiro, *Condorcet and the Rise of Liberalism*, p. 90.

16. Alphonse Aulard (1849-1928) was the first professional historian of the French Revolution, a subject to which he devoted his life. A professor at the University of Paris, his works include *Histoire politique de la Révolution française* from which the above quote is taken, and the nine-volume *Études et leçons sur la Révolution*. See Schapiro, *Condorcet and the Rise of Liberalism*, p. 91.

17. *Reflexions sur l'usufruit des bénéficiers*, X, 20. See J. Salwyn Schapiro, *Condorcet and the Rise of Liberalism*, p. 186.

18. *Sur l'admission des femines au droit de Cité*, X, 119-30.

19. Married women were deprived of the right to own property, retain earnings, share legal control over children and, of course, the means to correct these inequities, the right to vote.

20. The Nineteenth Amendment of the Constitution, providing, "The right of citizens of the United States to vote shall not be denied or abridged by the United States or by any State on account of sex," became operative on August 26, 1920.

21. *Le Républicain, ou Le défenseur du gouvernement representatif par une Société des républicains*. Four issues were published during July 1791.

22. This was the title bestowed upon Condorcet by the president of the electors of Paris when Condorcet was elected to the Legislative Assembly (Cahen, *Condorcet*, pp. 277-78). See Baker, *Condorcet*, pp. 304 and 464-65).

23. Schapiro, *Condorcet and the Rise of Liberalism*, p. 89.

24. J. Michelet, *Les femmes de la Révolution*, p. 86. See Schapiro, *Condorcet and the Rise of Liberalism*, pp. 89 and 289.

25. Condorcet selected the department of the Aisne (ibid., p. 95).

20

The Legislative Assembly

I

In its brief career from October 1, 1791, to September 20, 1792, the Legislative Assembly was preoccupied with the issue of war and then with its prosecution. As early as October 20, 1791, Jacques Pierre Brissot de Warville, better known as Brissot, the leader of the "Brissotins,"[1] had launched a campaign for war, denouncing the émigrés and calling for their expulsion from the territories around France. "In the event of a refusal," he told the Assembly, "you have no choice, you must yourselves attack the powers which dare to threaten you."[2]

The basis for Brissot's belligerence was the fact that Emperor Leopold of Austria, the brother of Marie-Antoinette, and the king of Prussia had threatened to restore Louis XVI to his prior position of power. Although the hatred so expressed was actual, the threat was a sham, since it was conditioned upon the cooperation of the other reigning monarchs of Europe.[3]

Nevertheless conflicting reasons motivated two essentially

antagonistic sources of power in France to agree on the promotion of the idea that war should be declared against Austria and Prussia.[4]

The advisors surrounding Louis XVI endorsed the idea because, they calculated, either defeat or victory would serve Louis well. On the one hand, the defeat of France in a war with Austria and Prussia would result, in their estimation, in the restoration of Louis to his former position of power, while victory for France in a war promoted by him could do no less, they expected, than to enhance his prestige. This, from their point of view, was a no-lose proposition.

Their antagonists in the Assembly, led by Brissot, reached the same conclusion by a different line of reasoning. Doubting Louis genuinely accepted his demotion in status from absolute monarch to constitutional monarch, they viewed war as a means of ending monarchy in France and of establishing a republican form of government both at home and abroad. One member of the Brissotin faction, Isnard of the Var, coined a slogan, "a war of peoples against kings," to express and justify that point of view.[5]

What was Condorcet's role in this crisis? On December 21, 1791, when Brissot "proposed an ultimatum to the Elector of Trier to disperse the armed émigrés gathering in his territory," Condorcet, in effect, seconded Brissot's proposal, by then proposing "the promulgation of an address solemnly declaring the principles and motives which have now brought the French nation to invoke 'the terrible right of war' in defense of its revolution."[6]

Robespierre was a strong minority dissenting voice, based on his view that war "might play into the hands of the king."[7] The duel between Brissot and Robespierre on the subject of war was the source of bitter differences between the two men and the factions they represented, leading ultimately to the victory of the Jacobins over the Girondists and the execution of Brissot in 1793 at the age of thirty-nine.

Initially, however, Brissot's position was the winning one. On April 20, 1792, the king presented a declaration of war to the Assembly and that body, in an outburst of patriotic enthusiasm, approved it with only seven dissenting votes. Unfortunately this war, which was so jubilantly and so nearly unanimously welcomed, was one that France was not prepared to wage, and the French army suffered immediate and serious reverses in the field.

Robespierre's fear that war might benefit the monarchy might have been realized had it not been for the occurrence of a mistake of major proportions in the strategy adopted by the émigrés. They persuaded the Duke of Brunswick, commander of the Prussian troops, to issue a manifesto on July 25, 1792, which threatened, in part, to wreak "a model vengeance" on Paris "never to be forgotten" if "the slightest outrage or violence is perpetrated against the royal family."[8] The manifesto was construed by the French as evidence of the king's disloyalty and support of the enemy. Instead of inspiring fear it energized their resistance and cemented the determination of the opponents of the monarchy to depose the king.

In Paris, the radicals proceeded to oust the regularly elected members of the Commune, to install their own representatives as the illegal but de facto rulers of Paris, and thus to instigate a municipal revolution.

August 10, 1792, was a fateful day in the history of France. On that day the long reign of the Bourbon kings of France came to an end, the Revolution began, and "the birth of the First French Republic was at hand."[9] It was on that day that an assault was launched upon the Tuileries, during which the king's Swiss guards were slaughtered. The king and the royal family were forced to flee for safety to the Legislative Assembly, which thereupon suspended the king from the performance of his functions. Two days later, the Assembly relinquished its control over the king and transferred him to the custody and less tender mercies of the Paris Commune,[10] a clear indication of the ascending power of the Commune. Recognizing the end of the constitutional monarchy and realizing its own futility, the Legislative Assembly ordered its own demise and the election of a successor convention by universal suffrage[11] for the purpose of adopting a constitution appropriate for a republic. The new assembly, called the National Convention, convened for the first time on September 21, 1792.

II

In the chaotic tumult of this major political and social revolution, the idealistic Condorcet was working on a report on the subject of education. But the violence and passion of the mob was quickly moving beyond the control of Condorcet and other rational voices. His education report was presented to the Assembly on the day it approved the declaration of war. In the excitement of the rising war hysteria, there was neither time nor thought for a report on education and it was promptly tabled. That was the unhappy end[12] of a work that in retrospect would be seen as one of Condorcet's great contributions.

The short life of the Legislative Assembly must have been a period of frustration for Condorcet, who was intent on bringing to the deliberations of a duly elected body of representatives of France the philosophes' point of view and the benefit of his experience and mature thought as their representative. This sense of obligation and opportunity as the last of the philosophes was expressed by him in a speech to the Parisian electors in which he said, "You have doubtless wished to honor in me the memory of the illustrious men whose friend I have had the happiness to be" and "to recompense them, in the person of a disciple whom they have loved, for all they have done to prepare and accelerate the reign of reason and liberty." Then he continued with this promise of dedication: "Faithful to their principles, it is in preserving the absolute independence of my opinions, in devoting all my care to seeking the truth and all my political action to declaring it, that I shall strive to respond to this glorious mark of your confidence."[13]

This sense of mission could not be fulfilled when war rather than political science was the dominant concern of the Legislative Assembly. Yet, while not successful immediately, Condorcet was able, through the opportunity of being a member of the Legislative Assembly, to exercise an important influence on education in France long after his death. Considering the significance and long-term effects of Condorcet's ideas on education, we should pause here in the narrative of the French Revolution to evaluate his contribution to educational reform.

Education in France had been largely limited to the upper classes through the end of the eighteenth century. It had not been regarded as a necessity for the peasants since literacy was not required for the performance of their occupations. Aulord, a renowned historian of the period, expresses the opinion that "eighty percent of the people of France could neither read nor write."[14] As late as 1763 a French writer, Louis-René Caradue de La Chalotais, in a work entitled *Essai d'education nationale* endorsed the idea that education should be limited to the minimal necessary for a man's occupation, since education in excess of that minimal amount "makes men discontent with their lot and disdainful of traditional occupations."[15] Strangely enough this was a point of view with which Voltaire agreed.[16]

To Condorcet, on the other hand, education was the key to enlightenment. It may not be an exaggeration to say that, in his mind education and enlightenment were synonymous. Accordingly, in his view, the establishment of a national and secular educational system of broad scope was a primary function of the state.

Prior to his election to the Legislative Assembly, Condorcet had written five *Memoires sur l'instruction publique*, published between January and September 1791. His tabled report on education to the Legislative Assembly, which he submitted as chairman of the Committee on Public Instruction, was entitled *Rapport et projet de décret sur l'organization générale de l'instruction publique*. Notably this title includes the theme of "general public instruction." The opening sentence of the report states, "Public education is a duty that society owes to all its citizens."[17]

Condorcet's theories about education gave recognition to the fact of intellectual differences in people while insisting upon the availability of educational facilities for all regardless of economic or social status. He predicated the need for universality of opportunity on two premises—that education is a natural right and that a healthy society cannot be partly educated and mostly uneducated. As he said,

> The wealthy classes could [not] continue to be enlightened if the masses were condemned to eternal stupidity. . . . It is when it spreads, not when it contracts that enlightenment becomes really effective. The more enlightenment is restricted to a few the greater is the danger that error will tarnish its brightness.[18]

Far in advance of his time, he applied these principles to women as well as to men. Condorcet was also a pioneer in his advocacy of adult education. It is interesting that he counseled coeducation in the primary grades. Despite his own status as a member of the nobility one of his reasons for the support of coeducation was the democratic idea that coeducation is a means of destroying aristocratic exclusivity. "A constitution which establishes political inequality will be neither durable nor desirable if it permits the existence of social institutions favorable to inequality."[19]

Another principle of Condorcet's educational proposal was that instructors and subject matter should be suitable for children of all faiths and therefore secular. For those reasons priests were to be forbidden to teach in public schools and moral instruction was to be totally separated from religious dogma. Since dogma, whether religious or political, was one of Condorcet's chief antipathies, one objective of the educational system he envisaged was to foster minds free of prejudices and open to the consideration of new ideas without being deterred by tradition or faith.

Condorcet's report on education was not limited to the philosophical ramifications of education in a democratic society; it also included carefully considered proposals regarding curriculum, scholarships, the training and selection of teachers, and other details of the practical operations of a national school system from primary to graduate school.

The subsequent and far-reaching influence of his thinking is reflected in the voice of a distinguished twentieth-century French statesman, Edouard Herriot (1872-1957), a man of letters and three-time premier of France, who said:

> There is no educational reformer in France who can afford to neglect this document in which is concentrated and epitomized

the best in the experience and in the revolutionary thought of the eighteenth century.[20]

The views of Condorcet in the eighteenth century became the inspiration and the model for education in France in the nineteenth and twentieth centuries. Incorporated in the French educational system as it developed were his ideas about secular education, compulsory and free elementary education, coeducation, adult education, a curriculum laced with instruction in the sciences and, ultimately, the extension of free education to the secondary level.

III

Besides the tabling of his splendid report on education, Condorcet had other causes for feeling frustrated as the lone philosophe in an assemblage of over seven hundred men comprising the Legislative Assembly, a constitutional body engaged in the task of directing the revolution by constitutional means. During the short period of its existence, the Legislative Assembly lost control of its destiny and became merely an ineffective debating society. Two events in the summer of 1792 served to diminish its authority almost to the point of extinction.

The issue upon which it floundered and finally lost its authority was the suspension of the king. A deeply divided Assembly was unable to reach a conclusion upon that question. The debate was continuous but fruitless. An impatient, unruly, and determined element of the Parisian populace, unhampered by the niceties of constitutional action and intent upon the resolution of the issue, took the matter into its own hands. On June 20, 1792, an armed mob invaded the meeting place of the

Legislative Assembly demanding action and then, moving on, proceeded to the Tuileries, invaded the royal palace and, while there, threatened and humiliated the king by "pinning" him "against a window seat for several hours."[21] Despite this warning the Assembly failed to resolve the issue.

Three weeks later, on August 10, 1792, rage and violence determined the issue. When the king fled for safety to the protective custody of the Legislative Assembly, after the massacre of his Swiss Guard, that body demonstrated its total loss of authority by promptly suspending the king and surrendering him to the custody of the illegal Paris Commune.

Most of the members of the right and center contingents, in disarray, were absent when the custody of the king was transferred. The remaining members, recognizing the end of the Legislative Assembly's authority, ordered the election of a constitutional convention by universal suffrage and charged it with the duty of adopting a constitution for the government of a republic.

Condorcet's role in this drama was ambivalent but logical. Motivated by the objective of ending the monarchy and establishing a republican form of government, he both encouraged and discouraged public clamor for action and change. On the one hand, he viewed popular pressure as a means of impelling the Assembly to end debate and take decisive action regarding the suspension of the king. On the other hand, the man of law, order, and reason within Condorcet recoiled from the idea of public action that disregarded and overrode representative government as a way of achieving a result.

Thus, the demonstration of public dissatisfaction with inaction that took place in the Tuileries on June 20, 1792, was approved by him as a positive popular demonstration likely to prompt decision by the Assembly instead of debate.[22] But the threat of insurrection that finally erupted on August 10 prompted Condorcet to say that "insurrection is the last word of oppressed people."[23] He "mourned deeply over the violations of the laws."[24] To no avail he urged the people to support and abide by representative government.

As the short career of the Assembly ended, Condorcet had some measure of satisfaction in the knowledge, despite his frustrations and failures of the Assembly, that he was still highly regarded as a thinker and a man of principle. The members of the Assembly listened to Condorcet with respect because they recognized that he was both incorruptible and irrevocably committed to the cause of liberty and the establishment of an enlightened and democratic government in France. Moreover he had the distinction of being the sole representative of the philosophes in their midst. To his voice and on his words "hung the Assembly, France and even Europe, eager to know how the friend of Voltaire, d'Alembert, and Turgot, judged the Revolution."[25] Five departments vied for the honor of naming him as their representative in the National Convention, the successor of the Legislative Assembly. From this wealth of recognition and offers, Condorcet selected the department of the Aisne as the department he represented in the last act of his career as legislator.

Notes

1. Brissot (1754–1793), the son of a restaurant owner in Chartres, is sometimes described as a lawyer—see William H. Harris and Judith S. Levey, eds., *The New Columbia Encyclopedia* (New York: Columbia University Press, 1975), p. 368—and sometimes as a lawyer's clerk— Alfred Cobban, *A History of Modern France,* vol. 1 (New York: Penguin, 1961), p. 185. Eventually he turned to journalism, becoming the founder

of the *Patriote Français* "which became one of the chief journals of the extreme revolutionaries" (ibid., pp. 185–86). In September 1791 he was elected to the Legislative Assembly where he became the leader of a faction of the Girondins known as the "Brissotins" (ibid., p. 186).

The Girondists, so named because the principal members of the original group were deputies of the Gironde department, were affiliated initially with the Jacobins. "Jacobins" was the name of a political club that derived its name from the monastery of the Jacobins in Paris where the members of the club met. "Jacobins," it might be noted, is the Parisian name of the Dominicans.

Ultimately, the more radical Jacobins dominated the Convention, the successor of the Legislative Assembly, and the Girondist leaders, including Brissot, were arrested and executed. After the fall of the Girondists in 1793, the Jacobins, led by Robespierre, instituted the "Reign of Terror," one of whose victims was Condorcet.

2. Ibid., pp. 189–90.

3. Ibid., p. 189.

4. Ibid., p. 190 and *The Columbia History of the World*, p. 768.

5. Cobban, *A History of Modern France*, vol. 1, p. 190. See also *The Columbia History of the World*, p. 768, and Keith M. Baker, *Condorcet: From Natural Philosophy to Social Mathematics* (Chicago: University of Chicago Press, 1982), p. 307.

6. Baker, *Condorcet*, p. 308.

7. Cobban, *A History of Modern France*, p. 190.

8. Crane Brinton et al., *A History of Civilization*, volume 2 (New York: Prentice Hall, 1976), p. 112.

9. Ibid.

10. Baker, *Condorcet*, p. 314.

11. According to Cobban, "the Convention . . . represented an effective vote of some 7.5 percent of the whole electorate." *A History of Modern France*, vol. 1, p. 203.

12. The subject of cost was considered and "postponed sine die" on May 25, 1791. See Baker, *Condorcet*, p. 466.

13. A quotation from C. Cahen's *Condorcet et la Revolution*

Française, p. 277, quoted by Keith M. Baker in *Condorcet*, pp. 306–307.

14. J. Salwyn Schapiro, *Condorcet and the Rise of Liberalism* (New York: Octagon, 1963), p. 197.

15. Baker, *Condorcet*, p. 289.

16. Ibid.

17. Shapiro, *Condorcet and the Rise of Liberalism*, p. 199.

18. *Assembliés provinciales*, VIII, 471. See Schapiro, *Condorcet and the Rise of Liberalism*, p. 200.

19. *Sur l'instruction publique*, VII, 223. Ibid., p. 202.

20. E. Herriot, *Créer* (Paris, 1920), vol. 2, p. 123. See Schapiro, *Condorcet and the Rise of Liberalism*, p. 198.

21. See Marcel Reinhard, *La Chute de la royalté*, pp. 313–30, and Baker, *Condorcet*, p. 309.

22. In his work on Condorcet, Baker says that "it is hardly surprising that, despite their implicit threat to the Assembly, Condorcet welcomed the events of 20 June as an unambiguous and dignified declaration of popular will," citing a comment by Condorcet in the *Chronique de Paris* of June 20, 1792, p. 693 (See Baker, *Condorcet*, p. 311).

23. *Chronique de Paris*, August 5, 1792, p. 869 (See Baker, *Condorcet*, pp. 313–14).

24. *Véritable et le faux ami du peuple I*, 602 (See Schapiro, *Condorcet and the Rise of Liberalism*, p. 94).

25. Schapiro, *Condorcet and the Rise of Liberalism*, p. 90.

21

The National Convention

I

The National Convention convened for the first time on September 21, 1792, ushering in the first year of the Republic. Of the three revolutionary assemblies, this was the most radical; it was committed to the end of the monarchy and the establishment of a republic. The deputies, about 750 in number, were divided into three groups reflecting the degree of their radical sentiments and differences in the character of their leaders. The center, also called the *pléin*, because it represented the majority (approximately 435), was the moderate group in this gatheing of radicals. On the right were the Girondists, about 165 in number, and, on the left, were about 150 Jacobins, a group also called the "mountain," because they sat high in the Assembly hall where they could look down on the others.[1]

The Girondist and Jacobin factions were closely related ideologically in their determination to change France to a republic and in a good deal of their philosophy about government and the rights of man. But two striking differences concerning the king, and a constitution for France separated them, as well as bitter personal animosities between their respective leaders, primarily Brissot, representing the Girondists, and Robespierre, representing the Jacobins. In addition they drew their strength from different constituencies whose objectives were in conflict at times. The Girondists came from and represented the provinces, whereas the Jacobins came from Paris and represented its interests. This was a crucial factor in their struggle for supremacy.[2]

Even though the Jacobins were the smallest faction, they dominated the Convention. This was due partly to the intensity of their drive for power and partly to their charismatic leader, the lawyer named Robespierre, whose personality was powerful, domineering, and fanatic in the pursuit of his objectives. But the main source of their strength came from the Commune of Paris and its radical population, which in moments of crisis gave the party immediate support.

A representative assembly should be a place for rational debate in which differences of opinion are freely expressed without fear of reprisal. But, as events developed, the business of the National Convention was conducted in an atmosphere marred not only by deeply bitter and jealous rivalries but by a psychology of violence, which was intolerant of differences and was ultimately committed to their resolution by the use of the guillotine.

The chain reaction of violence was begun by the Convention when the king, Louis XVI, was condemned to die and on January 21, 1792, he was subjected to the humiliating public spectacle of execution by guillotine—a shocking and gruesome display of the public's repudiation of a person who until recently had symbolized absolute rule by divine right. The dramatic fall from power made similar assaults on the persons of lesser prestige easier to carry out and to accept. In June 1793[3] twenty-nine

Girondin deputies, including Brissot,[4] were also consigned to the guillotine. Thus, the National Convention allegedly created to realize democratic ideals, stands out in history as a model of everything that a representative, deliberative assembly should not be, the participant in and promoter of a Reign of Terror.[5]

II

This was the vortex into which the eminently rational, scholarly, and gentle Condorcet was swept in September 1792 as the respected deputy from the department of the Aisne. He was totally misfitted, intellectually and temperamentally, for participation in legislative activity that was both irrational and violent.

His work for the Convention started out conventionally and auspiciously. Because of the eminence he had attained as a political scientist he was made chairman of the committee charged with the duty of preparing a new constitution for France. The other members of the committee deferred to him to such an extent that he was largely the author of the product that was submitted to the Convention for its approval. He poured into his draft of the constitution the results of all the years of study and thought he had given to the subject of the government of free people. Broadly stated the government of France he envisaged was a republic with legislative power vested in a popularly elected unicameral legislature and executive power vested in a popularly elected committee.

The finished draft reflected several concepts in Condorcet's thinking.

First and foremost was the establishment in the constitution of a bill of inalienable human rights. The draft submitted by Condorcet contained, therefore, as its introduction, a Declaration of Rights similar to the earlier Declaration of Rights of Man and Citizen.

Second was the creation of a governmental structure that would assure the recognition and protection of fundamental human rights and that would, as the representative of the people, effectuate their will. To that end his draft provided for a popularly elected unicameral legislature based on the premise that a bi-cameral legislature might lead to the creation of a second "Estate" which, like the First and Second Estates in French history, might represent special interests and might interfere with or impede legislation for the benefit of the people in favor of a select group.

Third, based on his knowledge of the history of France and a lifetime of experience with an absolute monarchy, his draft included provisions designed to prevent the excessive concen-tration of power. To that end he proposed a popularly elected executive committee instead of a single executive and, in addition, provision for local self-government to avoid the possibility of vesting too much power in a central authority located in Paris.

Despite Condorcet's dedication to women's suffrage, his pro-posal provided only for universal male suffrage, possibly because the other members of the constitutional committee persuaded him that France was not ready to accept so radical an innovation.[6]

The debate on his draft began in April 1793, some months after he had completed it. Evidently, Condorcet's presentation was ineffective. The draft was too lengthy and his delivery was unsuited for an assembly that was responsive to oratory designed to stir men to action. If he had been sitting at a table in a conference room where his intelligence, knowledge, and sincerity could have carried great weight, he might have succeeded. But in an assembly hall packed with excitable delegates with brief attention spans, he was completely out of his element.

It is probable that even if Condorcet had the voice and the magnetism of Winston Churchill, he could not have persuaded the convention to go along with him because of the intense rivalry between the Girondins and the Jacobins. Anything wearing the Girondin label would probably have been anathema to the Jacobins, and in their eyes Condorcet's draft constitution was a product of the Girondins, despite the fact that they knew that Condorcet was not a Girondin but his own man—an independent. Nevertheless, because the Girondins dominated the membership of the committee on the constitution and were the aggressive proponents of the adoption of Condorcet's draft, his draft was known as the Girondin constitution.[7] That, in the eyes of the Jacobins, was a fatal defect.

A serious point of debate between the two factions was the issue of centralized versus decentralized government. In an assembly of men in a rational state of mind, that was an issue that could have been argued, brought to a compromise, or put to a fair vote. But in the atmosphere of the Reign of Terror, intellectual arguments only masked underlying emotions of animosity and distrust. When the tug of war between the Girondins and the Jacobins was decided not by a vote but by the execution of the Girondin deputies, that, of course, was the end of Condorcet's draft. A Jacobin draft of the constitution that adopted many of Condorcet's ideas was quickly prepared, presented to the Convention, and adopted on June 24, 1793.

Condorcet was outraged by these events. Had he been more astute as a politician, he would not have made the mistake, in the climate of that period of the Revolution, of writing an anonymous pamphlet entitled "To French Citizens About the New Constitution," in which he excoriated the Jacobins for the expulsion and death of the Girondin deputies and denounced the Jacobin constitution.[8] The identity of the author of the pamphlet was promptly discovered. On July 8, 1793, a deputy named Chabot addressed the Convention, denounced Condorcet's pamphlet, and made a motion for his arrest. That motion was quickly granted. It was then that Condorcet fled to the shelter of Madame Vernet's pension to hide from his executioners and to write the "Last Will and Testament of the Eighteenth Century."

It is ironic that the French Revolution, while making possible the realization of the hopes of the philosophes for reform, at the same time brought to an end the Age of Reason. We may cite the summary execution of the Girondins and the death sentence imposed on Condorcet as the events marking the end of the Age of Reason and the beginning of the mindless Reign of Terror. The actions of Robespierre and the Jacobins suggest that they were implementing Rousseau's idea that in carrying out the general will, man can be forced to be free. In *The Social Contract*, it will be recalled, Rousseau said that the individual "shall be obliged to observe the general will" and that "this means nothing less than that he will be forced to be free"[9] (a conclusion that in my view disqualifies him as a philosophe).

One can sense the adoption of that philosophy in a speech made by Robespierre in February 1794. In the course of that speech, he said:

> What is the goal toward which we are striving? The peaceful enjoyment of liberty and equality: the rule of that eternal justice whose laws have been engraved . . . upon the hearts of men, even upon the heart of the slave who ignores them and of the tyrant who denies them.[10]

That is the expression of a noble ideal by a man who is nonetheless unperturbed by the summary expulsion and death of his colleagues because he feels that their condemnation was justified in the interest of promoting the general will and therefore warranted even if it forced men to be free by the fear of death.

Notes

1. See Crane Brinton et al., *A History of Civilization* (New York: Prentice-Hall, 1976), vol. 2, p. 114.

2. The Girondist party was so named because it centered around deputies from Bordeaux in the Gironde department.

3. See Alfred Cobban *A History of Modern France*, vol. 1: 1715–1799 (New York: Penguin, 1961), p. 225.

4. Jacques Pierre Brissot de Warville (1754–1793), a lawyer, was editor of the *Patriote français*, which became the organ of the Girondists and was initially called the Brissotine. See William H. Harris and Judith S. Levey, eds., *The New Columbia Encyclopedia* (New York: Columbia University Press, 1975), p. 368.

5. According to Alfred Cobban, *A History of Modern France*, p. 237, 300,000 people were put under arrest during the Terror, and of those who were guillotined, 85 percent belonged to the Third Estate, 6.5 percent belonged to the Clergy, and 8.5 percent belonged to the Noblesse. Brinton et al., in *A History of Civilization*, vol. 2, p. 116, say that 20,000 Frenchmen lost their lives during the Terror.

6. J. Salwyn Schapiro, in *Condorcet and the Rise of Liberalism* (New York: Octagon Press, 1963), p. 100, advances as a theory for the omission of women's suffrage in Condorcet's draft of the Constitution, that Condorcet "was disgusted when *la femme* appeared in the Fouhourriennes, or mobs of market women who were mobilized by Marat to disturb the sittings of the Convention." Keith M. Baker in *Condorcet: From Natural Philosophy to Social Mathematics* (Chicago: Chicago University Press, 1982), p. 321, takes the view that "it seems likely that the committee discussions had convinced him that the French were not yet ready to take such a step." That seems to me to be the more likely explanation for Condorcet's omission of the right of women to vote, since subsequently he forcefully advocated and predicted the adoption of women's suffrage in his *Sketch*.

7. Danton was the only Jacobin on the committee.

8. *Aux citoyens français sur la nouvelle constitution.*

9. *The Social Contract and Discourses*, rev. ed., trans. G. D. H. Cole (Rutland, Vt.: C. E. Tuttle, 1991, Everyman's Classic Library), Bk. 1, Ch. 8, p. 18.

10. *Le Moniteur Universal*, February 7, 1794. See C. Brinton et al., *A History of Civilization*, vol. 2, pp. 114–15.

Part Five

Sketch for a Historical Picture of the Progress of the Human Mind

22

The *Sketch* and Its Prediction of Progress

July 8, 1793, was the day that transformed Condorcet from a distinguished public figure into a criminal and a fugitive in fear for his life. On that day his strongly voiced opposition to the constitution that had been submitted to the Convention by the Jacobins and adopted by it was followed by an ominous order for his arrest. It was then that he fled to the sanctuary of Mme. Vernet's home.

Condorcet had good reason to fear for his life. The arrest warrant issued by the Convention was essentially equivalent to a decree of death, for it was issued during the intolerant and violent Reign of Terror period (June 1793 to July 1794), when dissent was treated as treason and execution was the approved prescription for its suppression.

But in this case the persecution of the dissenter had the uncommon effect of producing a good and lasting contribution. The *Sketch* was the creative climax of Condorcet's career. Its conception and writing was a last act, the influence of which has endured into the twentieth century and will probably continue in the future. This "last will and testament" preserved for posterity the lessons furnished by the experience of the eighteenth century, to be learned and relearned wherever and whenever the themes of equality, liberty, tolerance, and the progress of the open mind are threatened or their importance is forgotten.

One interesting but speculative question is whether Condorcet had the benefit of a reference library in Mme. Vernet's home in writing the *Sketch* or whether he composed it on the basis of his own knowlege, acquired through a lifetime of intellectual activity. The latter possibility is very plausible because Condorcet was both erudite and gifted with a prodigious memory.

The *Sketch*'s thesis regarding the progress of the human mind and the possibility of its perfectibility is based on two lines of argument, one historical, the other scientific.

On the historical level the *Sketch* is divided into nine chapters, each one of which is called a "Stage" in the progress and, at times, the retrogression of the mental development of the human race. The following are the nine "Stages" into which Condorcet divides history beginning with tribal society as the "First Stage," and concluding with French and Anglo-American society at the threshold of the nineteenth century as the "Ninth Stage":

The First Stage: "Men are united in tribes."

The Second Stage: "Pastoral peoples: The transition from this stage to that of agricultural peoples."

The Third Stage: "The progress of agricultural peoples up to the invention of the alphabet."

The Fourth Stage: "The progress of the human mind in Greece up to the division of the sciences about the time of Alexander the Great."

The Fifth Stage: "The progress of the sciences from their division to their decline."

The Sixth Stage: "The decadence of knowledge to its restoration about the time of the 'crusades.' "

The Seventh Stage: "The early progress of science from its revival in the West to the invention of printing."

The Eighth Stage: "From the invention of printing to the time when philosophy and the sciences shook off the yoke of authority."

The Ninth Stage: "From Descartes to the foundation of the French Republic."[1]

A final "Tenth Stage," unlike the first nine Stages, is addressed to prediction rather than history. It bears the subtitle "The Future Progress of the Human Mind." (See Appendix.)

Condorcet's account of our life on earth from its beginning in tribal society to the last decade of the eighteenth century is a very personal, very subjective reading of history, colored by his thesis and designed to establish two propositions: First, that the human mind has progressed, with some setbacks, from a state in which knowledge was primitive and ignorance, superstition, "religious servitude,"[2] and subservience to authority in thinking were the common condition, to a state of development that is highly sophisticated in knowledge and both independent and rational in thought.

Second, that "the perfectibility of man is truly indefinite," a word in Condorcet's usage, as noted, that is synonymous with infinite.[3] In his view, progress that has already been achieved toward perfection assures that "from now onwards independent of any power that might wish to halt it" there is no other limit "to that progress than the duration of the globe upon which nature has cast us."[4]

Thus, the basic premise of Condorcet's portrait of the history of the human mind is its gradual emancipation from servility to and domination by the authority of state and church and its achievement of liberation from the control of both institutions.

"Politics," he says at one point, "in deciding what was just, always respected whatever was consecrated by habit, ancient customs, and convention."[5] "Printing," he says at another point, "freed the education of the people from all religious shackles."[6] Above all, Condorcet argues, history demonstrates that the primary impediment to the development of the human mind has been the influence and restraint exercised by the establishments of religion. It is a theme that he stresses again and again. Typical of his opinion about the deterrent effect of ecclesiastics upon independent thinking is his pre-Orwellian comment regarding Socrates' mission in life—that he wanted men to think for themselves, but that "of all crimes it is this that priestly arrogance knows the least how to forgive."[7] In a later chapter, he says that religion, far from recognizing the authority of reason, claimed to overrule it and glorified in its humiliation."[8]

Thus, in his description of "The Fourth Stage," covering the golden age of Greek civilization, he ascribes the flowering of the human mind in that period to the fact that "the task of the priests was limited to the offices of religion" with the result that "genius could display itself to the full without submitting to pedantic regulation or to the hypocritical system of a seminary. . . . All men there had an equal right to know the truth [and] all could search for it and disseminate it to all in its entirety."[9]

On the other hand, in his account of "The Sixth Stage," a period when knowledge wanes before its restoration about the time of the crusades, he attributes the "rapid decline" of the human mind during "this disastrous stage" to "theological day-dreaming and superstitious imposture." Man's "only morality" was "religious intolerance."[10] This was a time when:

> People had so little idea of the method of proof by which matters of fact could be established that they found it simpler to ask heaven for a miracle whenever they wanted to distinguish the guilty from the innocent and the outcome of a superstitious trial by ordeal or the result of a duel were regarded as the surest methods of discovering and establishing the truth.[11]

It was in the "Seventh Stage,"[12] that, according to Condorcet, the great reversal occurred in the progress of the human mind. This reversal from subservience to authority in thinking to its liberation is attributed by him primarily to the introduction of printing into Western Europe by Gutenberg.[13] Through the spread of knowledge beyond the clergy and the stimulation of scientific discovery, it accomplished the deliverance of the human mind from the monopoly and control of thought by both state and church. It was then that human beings emerged from "their long lethargy."[14]

In Condorcet's presentation of history, it is in the "Ninth Stage," the period contemporary with his life, that the upward march and release of the human mind from the bonds that held it in check reached fruition in the American and French revolutions. He extolled the two revolutions, despite his own unhappy predicament as the result of one of them, because they had produced the practical realization of the philosophy of enlightenment by the recognition and adoption of the concepts of equality and liberty as natural rights and as princples of government. In his view they had achieved the truth that "the human mind" was "formed to be" free.[15]

Commenting on the American Revolution he says:

One nation alone escapes the two-fold influence of tyranny and superstition. From that happy land where freedom had only recently kindled the torch of genius, the mind of man released from the leading-strings of its infancy, advances with firm steps towards the truth.[16]

It is "the French and Anglo-American" societies that are "the most enlightened, the freest and least burdened by prejudices."[17]

Because English and French are the languages "most widely spoken" and are the languages of the two peoples who enjoy liberty to the fullest extent and who best understand its principles, we have no reason to fear, in Condorcet's opinion, that any "league of tyrants," or any "political intrigues, could prevent the resolute defense, in these two languages, of the rights of reason and of liberty."[18] This theme is carried forward in the following and final chapter of the *Sketch* in which Condorcet, at its very outset, asks this leading question: "Will all nations one day attain that state of civilization which the most enlightened, the freest and the least burdened by prejudices, such as the French and the Anglo-Americans have attained already?"[19] The answer to that question is set forth in the *Sketch*'s final chapter.

As envisioned by Condorcet, "The Tenth Stage" relates to a future in which the human mind, forever released by the revolutions in France and the United States from the tyrannies of religious intolerance and despotic government, achieves progress and moves onward toward perfection. In his treatment of the future, this "Stage" is both program and prediction concerning the upward movement of the race."[20]

To a considerable extent this portrayal of the times ahead is based on an analysis by Condorcet that is partly scientific and partly historical in character, in that it relates to the development of scientific knowledge, as distinguished from the history of our social and political development.[21] The renaissance of scientific knowledge begins, in Condorcet's account, with the introduction of printing by Gutenberg, as a result of which, as Condorcet said, "knowlege became the subject of a brisk and universal trade."[22] That "universal trade" led to the remarkable chain of discoveries by Newton, Leibniz, Huyghens, Kepler, Franklin, and others, which created "an imposing monument to the power of human intelligence."[23] The arts of architecture and medicine, as well as the various sciences such as astronomy, chemistry, and physics, shared the benefits of the wide dissemination of knowledge. A great burst of energy was released when the human mind was freed from the bonds that had held it in check such as the "prejudices of scholasticism."[24]

Based on the record of the political and social history of the human race and on the history of its scientific development, Condorcet stresses, the onward march of the human mind is an inexorable force that cannot be stopped by the exercise of any political or religious restraint.

To that argument he adds another based on the theory of probability. Among Condorcet's many works, one exercised a striking influence upon the views he later expressed in the *Sketch* about progress and perfectibility. It was an essay published in 1785, entitled "Essay on the Application of Analysis to the Probability of Majority Decisions,"[25] a work that occupies a place of distinction in the history of the theory of probabilities."[26]

Probability theory is addressed to the problem of analysis and the measurement of uncertainties, as, for example, in the determination of insurance premiums for the coverage of varieties of risk.[27] As *The Encyclopedia of Philosophy* says, "Anybody who aspires to rationality must be guided by probabilities in the face of uncertainty."[28] One method for the analysis of probabilities is the mathematics of calculus.[29]

Condorcet's essay on probabilities reflects his expertise as a mathematician applied to his interest in social and political problems. Through the calculus of probabilities, defined as "the mathematical doctrine and computation of the probabilities of events,"[30] he endeavored to establish that mathematical method can be applied to the solution of moral and political issues as well as to problems that are scientific in nature.

The "Tenth State," as a consequence, is laced with references to "the calculus of probablities."[31] While Condorcet conceded that the evaluations achieved in the social sciences may be less probable than the results accomplished in the physical sciences, he argued that the calculus of probabilities, nevertheless, provides a mathematical method of measuring probability in both branches of science. Accordingly he concludes in the "Tenth Stage" that "if man can with almost complete assurance, predict phenomena when he knows their laws . . . why . . . should it be regarded as a fantastic undertaking to sketch with some pretense to truth, the future destiny of man on the basis of history?"[32] To that rhetorical question he has this response:

> The sole foundation for belief in the natural sciences is this idea, that the general laws directing the phenomena of the universe, known or unknown, are necessary and constant—why should this principle be any less true for the development of the intellectual and moral faculties of man than for the operations of nature?[33]

These considerations lead to this conclusion: "We may conclude then that the perfectibility of man is indefinite."[34] Beneath this pattern of argument to support the prediction of the "ascent of man" is Condorcet's underlying confidence in the power of reason to propel the human mind forward and onward toward ultimate perfection through the exercise of rational and independent thought.

Some of the specific programs that Condorcet predicted in the course of the story of progress that he charts for the future in "The Tenth Stage" are remarkably prescient in the light of the actual historical development that has taken place since the end of the eighteenth century. In terms of our own development in the United States they include universal suffrage, universal education, the equivalents of social security, medicare and medicaid, and the achievement, in many aspects, of the movement for the equality of women. In short, looking forward, far in advance of his time, he foresaw the pattern of the modern, western, democratic welfare state and the then seemingly improbable liberation of women from centuries of political, economic, and social subordination.

Perhaps, in retrospect, the most impressive effect of the *Sketch* is the picture that it reveals of a man of reason, balanced judgment, and nobility of character. Despite the violent frenzy swirling about him and threatening his own life, he did not let it affect his appraisal of the development of the human mind or his vision of its future progress. His dispassionate reasoning was unclouded by anger, bitterness, or fear. Nowhere in the *Sketch* is there any mention of the Reign of Terror or of his own precarious situation. It is a fair inference from his silence regarding the violence from which he had fled that he considered it to be a temporary lapse, a moment only of retrogression in the inexorable forward march of humanity toward perfection and, therefore, unimportant in the portrayal of the larger picture of the development of the human mind.

It is only in the last paragraph of the *Sketch* that he permits himself a brief, general observation regarding the fact that philosophers must also be included among the victims of "the errors, crimes and injustices that still pollute the earth." Nevertheless, he concludes undaunted, it is the philosopher's reward for "his efforts to assist the progress of reason and the defense of liberty that he can contemplate the release of the human race from its shackles" and its advance "along the path of truth, virtue and happiness."[35]

That is the sanguine attitude and the calm voice of a man of reason calling to us in the twentieth century as he brings the Sketch to its end with his vision of the future. The Sketch is an unintended portrayal of greatness in character. Condorcet was not only an aristocrat socially. He was also an aristocrat in mind and in character.

The Convention must have recognized these qualities. Although it had issued the order for Condorcet's arrest, it reversed its mandate after his death and directed the publication of the Sketch.[36] Unwittingly it launched a trailblazer in the establishment of sociology as a social science. Today Condorcet is recognized as a pioneer and a founder of the science of society.[37]

The key word in the posthumous elevation of Condorcet from the status of philosophe to that of a founder of the science of society is progress. The idea of progress is so much a part of our thinking that it seems strange to relate that it has not always been so.

To depict the saga of the idea of progress in the briefest terms it may be summarized by noting that the Greeks and Romans looked back to a golden past from which, they thought, mankind had descended. In the Middle Ages, on the other hand, a bright future was not considered to be an earthly one but an escape from this life to a better life hereafter. The idea of progress, in short, is a modern one.[38] It was only in the sixteenth and seventeenth centuries, with the surge in scientific knowledge and the revelations of exploration, that the idea of progress began to take root.[39] Even as late as the middle of the eighteenth century, it will be recalled, Rousseau expressed the view, in writings that made him a celebrity, that the human race had had an idyllic past, which had been corrupted by art, literature, and printing. Nevertheless the prevailing optimism of the Age of Enlightenment and the enormous confidence of most eighteenth-century thinkers in the power of reason reversed the historical line of thought about a better past and made the idea of progress the accepted way of thinking about the future.

Condorcet made an enormously influential contribution with the *Sketch* to the acceptance of the idea of progress as a way of thinking based on the record of the past revealed by a study of history and on the basis of a scientific rationale. Although he did not have the benefit of Darwin's *Origin of Species,* he adopted an evolutionary approach in his analysis of the historical development of the human mind, leading to the concept that society is inevitably engaged in a continuing course of progress. He buttressed that concept by applying to social science the calculus of probabilities, as previously noted.

Almost two hundred years separate us in time from the last act of Condorcet's life. But a reading of the *Sketch* and reflection about the mind, character, and ideas of the man who wrote it lead to the conclusion that he was an intelligent, rational, reasonable, considerate, humane, broad-minded human being— the very model of a person to be admired and emulated. His character, his progressive ideas, many of which were far in advance of his time, and his influence upon later thinkers suggest that the last of the philosophes should be ranked with Voltaire, the first philosophe, as one of the greatest minds in the annals of history and one of its finest personalities.

Looking back from the perspective of the two hundred years that separate us from Condorcet's death, it can also be said that Benedetto Croce appraised the *Sketch* correctly when he called it the "Last Will and Testament of the Eighteenth Century." There is no better evidence of the truth of Croce's assessment than the fact that the National Convention, which had condemned Condorcet, reversed itself in 1795, one year after his death, and funded the printing of three thousand copies of the *Sketch* for distribution throughout France. In so doing, in one of its better, more reflective moments, it recognized the *Sketch* for what it was, the last, best expression of the ideas and ideals of the Enlightenment in the long struggle for emancipation and recognition of human rights.

Written in the closing days of a life and the closing years of the eighteenth century by the only philosophe to have lived under the rule of absolute monarchy and to have served in two of the revolutionary assemblies, the *Sketch* gave to posterity, as no other book did, a sense of the revolution that had occurred in both the recognition of human rights and the obligations of government to the people. It bequeathed for the consideration of future generations the ideas, aspirations, and hopes of the Enlightenment.

Writing in haste and in constant fear of discovery and death, conscious of the lack of time for the completion of a larger work about progress, Condorcet penned a short, hurried, urgent message to the future, to serve as both a warning and a prediction based on the history of the past. Supported by the actual experience and observation of a witness to the indignity of those whose expressions of thought were subject to censorship and whose persons were exposed to summary arrest and imprisonment, the *Sketch's* outline of the past was a bequest to the future of a lesson to be learned and remembered, the gift of reasoned confidence in the progress of the future.

Notes

1. See the chapter headings in *Sketch for a Historical Picture of the Progress of the Human Mind,* trans. June Barraclough (New York: Noonday Press, 1955; reprint—Westport, Conn.: Hyperion Press, 1979).
2. Ibid., p. 17.
3. Ibid., pp. 200 and 201.
4. Ibid., p. 4.
5. Ibid., p. 97.
6. Ibid., p. 102.
7. Ibid., p. 46.
8. Ibid., p. 97.
9. Ibid., p. 42.
10. Ibid., p. 77.
11. Ibid., p. 82.
12. Ibid., p. 89.
13. Referring to the invention of printing, Condorcet introduces his discussion of the "Eighth Stage" by saying that "it is indeed fortunate that nobody had suspected the full extent of future success, for priests and kings would surely have united to smother at birth an enemy who was to unmask and dethrone them." (Ibid., p. 99.)
14. Ibid.
15. Ibid., p. 123.
16. Ibid. Concerning the philosophical ideas of the Enlightenment, as treated by Condorcet, see, for example, the comments about liberty and natural rights at pp. 92, 109, 111, 113, and 168 of the Noonday/Hyperion edition. At page 93, referring to the Magna Carta and similar chapters, he says, "These are the originals of those declarations of the rights of man which all enlightened men to-day regard as the cornerstone of liberty."
17. Ibid., p. 173.
18. Ibid., p. 169.
19. Ibid., p. 173.
20. At page 175 of the Noonday/Hyperion edition, Condorcet says,

"If we glance at the state of the world today we see first of all that in Europe the principles of the French constitution are already those of all enlightened men. We see them too widely propagated, too seriously professed, for priests and despots to prevent their gradual penetration even into the hovels of their slaves; there they will soon awaken in these slaves the remnants of their common sense and inspire them with that smouldering indignation which not even constant humiliation and fear can smother in the soul of the oppressed."

21. The dual reliance upon social and political history on the one hand and the history of scientific development on the other is reflected in a paragraph in the last chapter of the *Sketch* where Condorcet says, "We shall find in the experience of the past, in the observation of the progress that the sciences and civilization have already made, in the analysis of the progress of the human mind and of the development of its faculties, the strongest reasons for believing that nature has set no limit to the realization of our hopes." (Ibid., p. 175.)

22. Ibid., p. 99.

23. Ibid., p. 149.

24. Ibid., p. 153.

25. "*Essai sur l'application de l'analyze a la probabilite des decisions rendue a la pluralite des voix.*" This essay was republished in a second edition in 1805 under the title of "*Élémens du calcul des probabilities et son application aux jeux de hasard a la loterie et aux judgement des hommes.*"

26. See William H. Harris and Judith Levey, eds., *New Columbia Encyclopedia* (New York: Columbia University Press, 1975), p. 622, and the *Encyclopaedia Britannica*, p. 1080.

27. The *New Columbia Encyclopedia*, p. 16, defines an actuary as "one who calculates the probabilities involved in any contingency for which insurance is desired and establishes the premium necessary to cover such contingency."

28. Paul Edwards, ed., *The Encyclopedia of Philosophy* (Free Press, 1973), vol. 6, p. 464.

29. Calculus is defined as "the branch of mathematics that studies

continuously changing conditions" (*New Columbia Encyclopedia*, p. 420). The *Random House Dictionary of the English Language* defines calculus as "a method of calculation, esp. one of several highly systematic methods of treating problems by a special system of algebraic notations as differential, integral or infinitesimal calculus."

30. Webster's *New International Dictionary*, 2nd ed., unabridged.

31. *Sketch* (Noonday/Hyperion edition), pp. 181, 182, 190, 191.

32. Ibid., p. 173.

33. Ibid.

34. Ibid., p. 199.

35. Ibid., p. 201.

36. The *Sketch* was first published by order of the Convention in 1795 in an edition of three thousand copies with funds provided by the Convention. See the Noonday/Hyperion edition, p. xiii; J. S. Schapiro, *Condorcet and the Rise of Liberalism* (New York: Octagon, 1963), p. 107; Keith M. Baker, *Condorcet: From Natural Philosophy to Social Mathematics* (Chicago: Chicago University Press, 1982), p. 343.

37. For example, Samuel Koenig says, in *Sociology, an Introduction to the Science of Society* (Barnes & Noble), that "Condorcet anticipated the 'first' sociologist, Comte." (p. 23) and that the *Sketch* "formulated a theory of social change which had a far-reaching influence upon later sociological theories" (p. 13). Comte said, "From the beginning of my career I have never ceased to respect the great Condorcet as my spiritual father." (*Système de politique positive*, 5th ed. [Paris, 1929], vol. 3, xv–xvi.)

38. The introductory sentence of the *Encyclopedia of Philosophy* on the subject of the Idea of Progress states the proposition in this way: "In broad terms a popular belief in progress means the rejection of an attitude that has characterized most human communities throughout history" (vol. 6, p. 482).

39. The discovery of the Americas and their "savage" inhabitants gave credence to the idea that people had progressed from an earlier primitive stage to a more advanced state of "civilized" society.

Appendix

THE TENTH STAGE

The Future Progress of the Human Mind
[The Final Chapter of the *Sketch*]

If man can predict phenomena with almost complete assurance, when he knows their laws, and if, even when he does not, he can, with great expectation of success, still forecast the future on the basis of his experience of the past, why, then, should it be regarded as a fantastic undertaking to sketch, with some pretense to truth, the future destiny of man on the basis of his history? The sole foundation for belief in the natural sciences is the idea that the general laws directing the phenomena of the universe, known or unknown, are necessary and constant. Why should this principle be any less true for the development of the intellectual and moral faculties of man than for the other operations of nature? Since beliefs founded on past experience of like conditions provide the only rule of conduct for the wisest of men, why should the philosopher be precluded from having his conjectures on these same foundations, so long as he does not attribute to them a certainty superior to that warranted by the number, the constancy, and the accuracy of his observations?

Our hopes for the future condition of the human race can be subsumed under three important headings: (1) the abolition of inequality between nations, (2) the progress of equality within each nation, and (3) the true perfection of mankind. Will all nations one day attain that state of civilization which the most enlightened, the freest and the least burdened by prejudices, such as the French and the Anglo-Americans, have attained already? Will the vast gulf that separates these peoples from the slavery of nations under the rule of monarchs, from the barbarism of African tribes, from the ignorance of savages, little by little disappear?

Is there upon the face of the earth a nation whose inhabitants have been debarred by nature herself from the enjoyment of freedom and the exercise of reason?

Are the differences which have hitherto been seen in every civilized country in respect of the enlightenment, the resources, and the wealth enjoyed by the different classes into which it is divided, is that inequality between men which was aggravated or perhaps produced by the earliest progress of society, are these part of civilization itself, or are they due to the present imperfections of the social art? Will they necessarily decrease and ultimately make way for a real equality, the final end of the social art, in which even the effects of the natural differences between men will be mitigated and the only kind of inequality to persist will be that which is in the interests of all and which favors the progress of civilization, of education, and of industry, without entailing either poverty, humiliation, or dependence? In other words, will men approach a condition in which everyone will have the knowledge necessary to conduct himself in the ordinary affairs of life, according to the light of his own reason, to preserve his mind free from prejudice, to understand his rights and to exercise them in accordance with his conscience and his creed; in which everyone will become able, through the development of his faculties, to find the means of providing for his needs; and in which at last misery and folly will be the exception, and no longer the habitual lot of a section of society?

Is the human race to better itself, either by discoveries in the sciences and the arts, and so in the means to individual welfare and general prosperity; or by progress in the principles of conduct or practical morality; or by a true perfection of the intellectual, moral, or physical faculties of man, an improvement which may result from a perfection either of the instruments used to heighten the intensity of these faculties and to direct their use or of the natural constitution of man?

In answering these three questions we shall find in the experience of the past, in the observation of the progress that the sciences and civilization have already made, in the analysis of the progress of the human mind and of the development of its faculties, the strongest reasons for believing that nature has set no limit to the realization of our hopes.

If we glance at the state of the world today we see first of all that in Europe the principles of the French constitution are already those of all enlightened men. We see them too widely propagated and too seriously professed, for priests and despots to prevent their gradual penetration even into the hovels of their slaves; there they will soon awaken in these slaves the remnants of their common sense and inspire them with that smouldering indignation which not even constant humiliation and fear can smother in the soul of the oppressed.

As we move from nation to nation, we can see in each what special obstacles impeded this revolution and what attitudes of mind favor it. We can distinguish the nations where we may expect it to be introduced gently by the perhaps belated wisdom of their governments, and those nations where its violence intensified by their resistance must involve all alike in a swift and terrible convulsion.

Can we doubt that either common sense or the senseless discords of European nations will add to the effects of the slow but inexorable progress of their colonies, and will soon bring about the independence of the New World? And then will not the European population in these colonies, spreading rapidly over that enormous land, either civilize or peacefully remove the savage nations who still inhabit vast tracts of its land?

Survey the history of our settlements and commercial undertakings in Africa or in Asia. You will see how our trade monopolies, our treachery, our murderous contempt for men of another color or creed,

the insolence of our usurpations, the intrigues or the exaggerated prose-
lytic zeal of our priests have destroyed the respect and goodwill that
the superiority of our knowledge and the benefits of our commerce
at first won for us in the eyes of the inhabitants. Doubtless the moment
approaches when, no longer presenting ourselves as always either tyrants or corrupters, we shall become for them the beneficent instruments of their freedom.

The sugar industry, establishing itself throughout the immense
continent of Africa, will destroy the shameful exploitation which has
corrupted and depopulated that continent for the last two centuries.

In Great Britain, friends of humanity already have set us an example.
If the Machiavellian government of that country has been restrained
by public opinion from offering any opposition, what may we not expect
of this same spirit, once the reform of a servile and venal constitution
has led to a government worthy of a humane and generous nation?
Will not France hasten to imitate such undertakings dictated by
philanthropy and the true self-interest of Europe alike? Trading stations
have been set up in the French islands, in Guiana, and in some English
possessions, and soon we shall see the downfall of the monopoly that
the Dutch have sustained with so much treachery, persecution, and
crime. The nations of Europe will finally learn that monopolistic
companies are nothing more than a tax imposed upon them in order
to provde their governments with a new instrument of tyranny.

The peoples of Europe, confining themselves to free trade, understanding their own rights too well to show contempt for those of other
peoples, will respect this independence, which until now they have
so insolently violated. Their settlements, no longer filled with government hirelings hastening, under the cloak of place or privilege, to amass
treasure by brigandry and deceit, so as to be able to return to Europe
and purchase titles and honor, will now be peopled with men of indus-
trious habit, seeking in these propitious climates the wealth that eluded
them at home. The love of freedom will retain them there, ambition
will no longer recall them, and what have been no better than the
counting-houses of brigands will become colonies of citizens propagating

throughout Africa and Asia the principles and the practice of liberty, knowledge, and reason that they have brought from Europe. We shall see the monks, who brought only shameful superstition to these peoples and aroused their antagonism by the threat of yet another tyranny, replaced by men occupied in propagating among them the truths that will promote their happiness and in teaching them about their interest and their rights. Zeal for the truth is also one of the passions, and it will turn its efforts to distant lands, once there are no longer at home any crass prejudices to combat, any shameful errors to dissipate.

These vast lands are inhabited partly by large tribes who need only assistance from us to become civilized, who wait only to find brothers among the European nations to become their friends and pupils; partly by races oppressed by sacred despots or dull-witted conquerors, and who for so many centuries have cried out to be liberated; partly by tribes living in a condition of almost total savagery in a climate whose harshness repels the sweet blessings of civilization and deters those who would teach them its benefits; and finally, by conquering hordes who know no other law but force, no other profession but piracy. The progress of these two last classes of people will be slower and stormier; and perhaps it will even be that, reduced in number as they are driven back by civilized nations, they will finally disappear imperceptibly before them or merge into them.

We shall point out how these events will be the inevitable result not merely of the progress of Europe but also of the freedom that the French and the North American Republics can, and in their own real interest should, grant to the trade of Africa and Asia; and how they must of necessity be born either of a new-found wisdom on the part of the European nations, or of their obstinate attachment to mercantilist prejudices.

We shall show that there is only one event, a new invasion of Asia by the Tartars, that could prevent this revolution, and that this event is now impossible. Meanwhile everything forecasts the imminent decadence of the great religions of the East, which in most countries have been made over to the people, and, not uncontaminated by the corruption of their ministers, are in some already regarded by the ruling classes as mere political inventions; in consequence of which they are now powerless to retain human reason in hopeless bondage, in eternal infancy.

The progress of these peoples is likely to be more rapid and certain than our own because they can receive from us everything that we have had to find out for ourselves, and in order to understand those simple truths and infallible methods which we have acquired only after long error, all that they need to do is to follow the expositions and proofs that appear in our speeches and writings. If the progress of the Greeks was lost to later nations, this was because of the absence of any form of communication between the different peoples, and for this we must blame the tyrannical domination of the Romans. But when mutual needs have brought all men together, and the great powers have established equality between societies as well as between individuals and have raised respect for the independence of weak states and sympathy for ignorance and misery to the rank of political principles, when maxims that favor action and energy have ousted those which would compress the province of human faculties, will it then be possible to fear that there are still places in the world inaccessible to enlightenment, or that despotism in its pride can raise barriers against truth that are insurmountable for long?

The time will therefore come when the sun will shine only on free men who know no other master but their reason; when tyrants and slaves, priests and their stupid or hypocritical instruments will exist only in works of history and on the stage; and when we shall think of them only to pity their victims and their dupes; to maintain ourselves in a state of vigilance by thinking on their excesses; and to learn how to recognize and so to destroy, by force of reason, the first seeds of tyranny of superstition, should they ever dare to reappear among us.

In looking at the history of societies we shall have had occasion to observe that there is often a great difference between the rights that the law allows its citizens and the rights that they actually enjoy, and, again, between the equality established by political codes and that which in fact exists among individuals: and we shall have noticed that these differences were one of the principal causes of the destruction of freedom in the ancient republics, of the storms that troubled them, and of the weakness that delivered them over to foreign tyrants.

These differences have three main causes: (1) inequality in wealth; (2) inequality in status between the man whose means of subsistence are hereditary and the man whose means are dependent on the length of his life, or, rather, on that part of his life in which he is capable of work; and, finally, (3) inequality in education.

We therefore need to show that these three sorts of real inequality must constantly diminish without however disappearing altogether; for they are the result of natural and necessary causes which it would be foolish and dangerous to wish to eradicate; and one could not even attempt to bring about the entire disappearance of their effects without introducing even more fecund sources of inequality, without striking more direct and more fatal blows at the rights of man.

It is easy to prove that wealth has a natural tendency to equality, and that any excessive disproportion could not exist or at least would rapidly disappear if civil laws did not provide artificial ways of perpetuating and uniting fortunes; if free trade and industry were allowed to remove the advantages that accrued wealth derives from any restrictive law or fiscal privilege; if taxes on covenants, the restrictions placed on their free employment, their subjection to tiresome formalities and the uncertainty and inevitable expense involved in implementing them did not hamper the activity of the poor man and swallowed up his meager capital; if the administration of the country did not afford some men ways of making their fortune that were closed to other citizens; if prejudice and avarice, so common in old age, did not preside over the making of marriages; and if, in a society enjoying simpler manners and more sensible institutions, wealth ceased to be a means of satisfying vanity and ambition, and if the equally misguided notions of austerity, which condemn spending money in the cultivation of the more delicate pleasures, no longer insisted on the hoarding of all one's earnings.

Let us turn to the enlightened nations of Europe, and observe the size of their present populations in relation to the size of their territories. Let us consider in agriculture and industry the proportion that holds between labor and the means of subsistence, and we shall see that it would be impossible for those means to be kept at their present level and consequently for the population to be kept at its present size if a great number of individuals were not almost entirely dependent for the maintenance of themselves and their family either on their own labor or on the interest from capital invested so as to make their labor more productive. Now both these sources of income depend on the life and even on the health of the head of the family. They provide what is rather like a life annuity, save that it is more dependent on chance; and in consequence there is a very real difference between people living like this and those whose resources are not at all subject to the same risks, who live either on revenue from land, or on the interest on capital which is almost independent of their own labor.

Here then is a necessary cause of inequality, of dependence, and even of misery, which ceaselessly threatens the most numerous and most active class in our society.

We shall point out how it can be in great part eradicated by guaranteeing people in old age a means of livelihood produced partly by their own savings and partly by the savings of others who make the same outlay, but who die before they need to reap the reward; or, again, on the same principle of compensation, by securing for widows and orphans an income which is the same and costs the same for those families which suffer an early loss and for those which suffer it later; or again by providing all children with the capital necessary for the full use of their labor, available at the age when they start work and found a family, a capital that increases at the expense of those whom premature death prevents from reaching this age. It is to the application of the calculus to the probabilities of life and the investment of money that we owe the idea of these methods which have already been successful, although they have not been applied in a sufficiently comprehensive and exhaustive fashion to render them really useful, not merely to a few individuals, but to society as a whole, by making it possible to prevent those periodic disasters which strike at so many families and which are such a recurrent source of misery and suffering.

We shall point out that schemes of this nature, which can be organized in the name of the social authority and become one of its greatest benefits, can also be the work of private associations, which will be formed without any real risk, once the principles for the proper working of these schemes have been widely diffused and the mistakes which have been the undoing of a large number of these associations no longer hold terrors for us.

We shall reveal other methods of ensuring this equality, either by seeing that credit is no longer the exclusive privilege of great wealth, but that it has another and no less sound foundation; or by making industrial progress and commercial activity more independent of the existence of the great capitalists. And once again, it is to the application of the calculus that we shall be indebted for such methods.

The degree of equality in education that we can reasonably hope to attain, but that should be adequate, is that which excludes all dependence, either forced or voluntary. We shall show how this condition can be easily attained in the present state of human knowledge even by those who can study only for a small number of years in childhood, and then during the rest of their lives in their few hours of leisure. We shall prove that, by a suitable choice of syllabus and of methods of education, we can teach the citizen everything that he needs to know in order to be able to manage his household, administer his affairs, and employ his labor and his faculties in freedom; to know his rights and to be able to exercise them; to be acquainted with his duties and fulfill them satisfactorily; to judge his own and other men's actions according to his own lights and to be a stranger to none of the high and delicate feelings which honor human nature; not to be in a state of blind dependence upon those to whom he must entrust his affairs or the exercise of his rights; to be in a proper condition to choose and supervise them; to be no longer the dupe of those popular errors which torment man with superstitious fears and chimerical hopes; to defend himself against prejudice by the strength of his reason alone; and, finally, to escape the deceits of charlatans who would lay snares for his fortune, his health, his freedom of thought and his conscience under the pretext of granting him health, wealth, and salvation.

From such time onward the inhabitants of a single country will no longer be distinguished by their use of a crude or refined language; they will be able to govern themselves according to their own knowledge; they will no longer be limited to a mechanical knowledge of the procedures of the arts of professional routine; they will no longer depend for every trivial piece of business, every insignificant matter of instruction on clever men who rule over them in virtue of their necessary superiority; and so they will attain a real equality, since differences in enlightenment or talent can no longer raise a barrier between men who understand each other's feelings, ideas, and language, some of whom may wish to be taught by others but, to do so, will have no need to be controlled by them, or who may wish to confide the care of government to the ablest of their number but will not be compelled to yield them absolute power in a spirit of blind confidence.

This kind of supervision has advantages even for those who do not exercise it, since it is employed for them and not against them. Natural differences of ability between men whose understanding has not been cultivated give rise, even in savage tribes, to charlatans and dupes, to clever men and men readily deceived. These same differences are truly universal, but now they are differences only between men of learning and upright men who know the value of learning without being dazzled by it; or between talent or genius and the common sense which can appreciate and benefit from them; so that even if these natural differences were greater and more extensive than they are, they would be only the more influential in improving the relations between men and promoting what is advantageous for their independence and happiness.

These various causes of equality do not act in isolation; they unite, combine, and support each other and so their cumulative effects are stronger, surer, and more constant. With greater equality of education there will be greater equality in industry and so in wealth; equality in wealth necessarily leads to equality in education, and equality between the nations and equality within a single nation are mutually dependent.

We might say that a well-directed system of education rectifies natural inequality in ability instead of strengthening it, just as good laws remedy natural inequality in the means of subsistence, and just as in societies where laws have brought about this same equality, liberty, though subject to a regular constitution, will be more widespread, more complete than in the total independence of savage life. Then the social art will have fulfilled its aim, that of assuring and extending to all men enjoyment of the common rights to which they are called by nature.

The real advantages that should result from this progress, of which we can entertain a hope that is almost a certainty, can have no other term that that of the absolute perfection of the human race; since, as the various kinds of equality come to work in its favor by producing ampler sources of supply, more extensive education, more complete liberty, so equality will be more real and will embrace everything which is really of importance for the happiness of human beings.

It is therefore only by examining the progress and the laws of this perfection that we shall be able to understand the extent or the limits of our hopes.

No one has ever believed that the mind can gain knowledge of all the facts of nature or attain the ultimate means of precision in the measurement or in the analysis of the facts of nature, the relations between objects, and all the possible combinations of ideas. Even the relations between magnitudes, the mere notion of quantity or extension, taken in its fullest comprehension, gives rise to a system so vast that it will never be mastered by the human mind in its entirety, that there will always be a part of it, always indeed the larger part of it that will remain forever unknown. People have believed that man can never know more than a part of the objects that the nature of his intelligence allows him to understand, and that he must in the end arrive at a point where the number and complexity of the objects that he already knows have absorbed all his strength so that any further progress must be completely impossible.

But since, as the number of known facts increases, the human mind learns how to classify them and to subsume them under more general facts, and, at the same time, the instruments and methods employed in their observation and their exact measurement acquire a new precision; since, as more relations between various objects become known, man is able to reduce them to more general relations, to express them more simply, and to present them in such a way that it is possible to grasp a greater number of them with the same degree of intellectual ability and the same amount of application; since, as the mind learns to understand more complicated combinations of ideas, simpler formulae soon reduce their complexity; so truths that were discovered only by great effort, that could at first only be understood by men capable of profound thought, are soon developed and proved by methods that are not beyond the reach of common intelligence. If the methods which have led to these new combinations of ideas are ever exhausted, if their application to hitherto unsolved questions should demand exertions greater than either the time or the capacity of the learned would permit, some method of a greater generality or simplicity will be found so that genius can continue undisturbed on its path. The strength and the limits of man's intelligence may remain unaltered; and yet the instruments that he uses will increase and improve, the language that fixes and determines his ideas will acquire greater breadth and precision and, unlike mechanics where an increase of force means a decrease of speed, the methods that lead genius to the discovery of truth increase at once the force and the speed of its operations.

Therefore, since these developments are themselves the necessary consequences of progress in detailed knowledge, and since the need for new methods in fact only arises in circumstances that give rise to new methods, it is evident that, within the body of the sciences of observations, calculation, and experiment, the actual number of truths may always increase, and that every part of this body may developed, and yet man's faculties be of the same strength, activity, and extent.

If we apply these general reflections to the various sciences, we can find in each of them examples of progressive improvement that will remove any doubts about what we may expect for the future. We shall point out in particular the progress that is both likely and imminent in those sciences which prejudice regards as all but exhausted. We shall give examples of the manner and extent of the precision and unity which could accrue to the whole system of human knowledge as the result of a more general and philosophical application of the sciences of calculation to the various branches of knowledge. We shall show how favorable to our hopes would be a more universal system of education by giving a greater number of people the elementary knowledge which could awaken their interest in a particular branch of study, and by providing conditions favorable to their progress in it; and how these hopes would be further raised, if more men possessed the means to devote themselves to these studies, for at present even in the most enlightened countries scarcely one in fifty of the people who have natural talents receives the necessary education to develop them; and how, if this were done there would be a proportionate increase in the number of men destined by their discoveries to extend the boundaries of science.

We shall show how this equality in education and the equality which will come about between the different nations would accelerate the advance of these sciences whose progress depends on repeated observations over a large area; what benefits would thereby accrue to mineralogy, botany, zoology, and meteorology; and what a vast disproportion holds in all these sciences between the poverty of existing methods, which have nevertheless led to useful and important new truths, and the wealth of those which man would then to able to employ.

We shall show how even the sciences in which discovery is the fruit of solitary meditation would benefit from being studied by a greater number of people, in the matter of those improvements in detail which do not demand the intellectual energy of an inventor but suggest themselves to mere reflection.

If we turn now to the arts, whose theory depends on these same sciences, we shall find that their progress depending as it does on that of theory, can have no other limits; that the procedures of the different arts can be perfected and simplified in the same way as the methods of the sciences; new instruments, machines, and looms can add to man's strength and can improve at once the quality and the accuracy of his productions, and can diminish the time and labor that has to be expended on them. The obstacles still in the way of this progress will disappear, accidents will be foreseen and prevented, the unsanitary conditions that are due either to the work itself or to the climate will be eliminated.

A very small amount of ground will be able to produce a great quantity of supplies of greater utility or higher quality; more goods will be obtained for a smaller outlay; the manufacture of articles will be achieved with less waste of raw materials and will make better use of them. Every type of soil will produce those things which satisfy the greatest number of needs; of several alternative ways of satisfying needs of the same order, that will be chosen which satisfies the greatest number of people and which requires least labor and least expenditure. So, without the need for sacrifice, methods of preservation and economy in expenditure will improve in the wake of progress in the arts of producing and preparing supplies and making articles from them.

Not only will the same amount of ground support more people, but everyone will have less work to do, will produce more, and satisfy his wants more fully.

With all this progress in industry and welfare which establishes a happier proportion between men's talents and their needs, each successive generation will have larger possessions, either as a result of this progress or through the preservation of the products of industry; and so, as a consequence of the physical constitution of the human race, the number of people will increase. Might there not then come a moment when these necessary laws begin to work in a contrary direction; when, the number of people in the world finally exceeding the means of subsistence, there will in consequence ensue a continual diminution of happiness and population, a true retrogression, or at best an oscillation between good and bad? In societies that have reached this stage will not this oscillation be a perennial source of more or less periodic disaster? Will it not show that a point has been attained beyond which all further improvement is impossible, that the perfectibility of the human race has after long years arrived at a term beyond which it may never go?

There is doubtless no one who does not think that such a time is still very far from us; but will it ever arrive? It is impossible to pronounce about the likelihood of an event that will occur only when the human species will have necessarily acquired a degree of knowledge of which we can have no inkling. And who would take it upon himself to predict the condition to which the art of converting the elements to the use of man may in time be brought?

Even if we agree that the limit will one day arrive, nothing follows from it that is in the least alarming as far as either the happiness of the human race or its indefinite perfectibility is concerned; if we consider that, before all this comes to pass, the progress of reason will have kept pace with that of the sciences, and that the absurd prejudices of superstition will have ceased to corrupt and degrade the moral code by its harsh doctrines instead of purifying and elevating it, we can assume that by then men will know that, if they have a duty toward those who are not yet born, that duty is not to give them existence but to give them happiness; their aim should be to promote the general welfare of the human race or of the society in which they live or of the family to which they belong, rather than foolishly to encumber the world with useless and wretched beings. It is, then, possible that there should be a limit to the amount of food that can be produced, and, consequently, to the size of the population of the world, without this involving that untimely destruction of some of those creatures who have been given life, which is so contrary to nature and to social prosperity.

Since the discovery, or rather the exact analysis of the first principles of metaphysics, morals, and politics is still recent and was preceded by the knowledge of a large number of detailed truths, the false notion that they have thereby attained their destination, has gained ready acceptance; men imagine that, because there are no more crude errors to refute, no more fundamental truths to establish, nothing remains to be done.

It is easy to see how imperfect is the present analysis of man's moral and intellectual faculties; how much further the knowledge of his duties, which presumes a knowledge of the influence of his actions upon the welfare of his fellow men and upon the society to which he belongs, can still be increased through a more profound, more accurate, more considered observation of that influence; how many questions have to be solved, how many social relations to be examined, before we can have precise knowledge of the individual rights of man and the rights that the state confers upon each in regard to all. Have we yet ascertained at all accurately the limits of the rights that exist between different societies in times of war, or that are enjoyed by society over its members in times of trouble and schism, or that belong to individuals, or spontaneous associations at the moment of their original, free formation or of their necessary disintegration?

If we pass on to the theory which ought to direct the application of particular principles and serve as the foundation for the social art, do we not see the necessity of acquiring a precision that these elementary truths cannot possess so long as they are absolutely general? Have we yet reached the point when we can reckon as the only foundation of law either justice or a proved and acknowledged utility instead of the vague, uncertain, arbitrary views of alleged political expediency? Are we yet in possession of any precise rules for selecting out of the almost infinite variety of possible systems in which the general principles of equality and natural rights are respected, those which will best secure the preservation of these rights, which will afford the freest scope for their exercise and their enjoyment, and which will moreover insure the leisure and welfare of individuals and the strength, prosperity, and peace of nations?

The application of the calculus of combinations and probabilities to these sciences promises even greater improvement, since it is the only way of achieving results of an almost mathematical exactitude and of assessing the degree of their probability or likelihood. Sometimes, it is true, the evidence upon which these results are based may lead us, without any calculation, at the first glance, to some general truth and teach us whether the effect produced by such-and-such a cause was or was not favorable, but if this evidence cannot be weighed and measured, and if these effects cannot be subjected to precise measurement, then we cannot know exactly how much good or evil they contain; or, again, if the good and evil nearly balance each other, if the difference between them is slight, we cannot pronounce with any certainty to which side the balance really inclines. Without the application of the calculus it would be almost impossible to choose with any certainty between two combinations that have the same purpose and between which there is no apparent difference in merit. Without the calculus these sciences would always remain crude and limited for want of instruments delicate enough to catch the fleeting truth, of machines precise enough to plumb the depths where so much that is of value to science lies hidden.

However, such an application, notwithstanding the happy efforts of certain geometers, is still in its earliest stages, and it will be left to the generations to come to use this source of knowledge which is as inexhaustible as the calculus itself, or as the number of combinations, relations, and facts that may be included in its sphere of operation.

There is another kind of progress within the sciences that is no less important; and that is the perfection of scientific language which is at present so vague and obscure. This improvement could be responsible for making the sciences genuinely popular, even in their first rudiments. Genius can triumph over the inexactitude of language as over other obstacles and can recognize the truth through the strange mask that hides or disguises it. But how can someone with only a limited amount of leisure to devote to his education master and retain even the simplest truths if they are distorted by an imprecise language? The fewer the ideas that he is able to acquire and combine, the more necessary is it that they should be precise and exact. He has no fund of knowledge stored up in his mind which he can draw upon to protect himself from error, and his understanding, not being strengthened and refined by long practice, cannot catch such feeble rays of light as manage to penetrate the obscurities, the ambiguities of an imperfect and perverted language.

Until men progress in the practice as well as in the science of morality, it will be impossible for them to attain any insight into either the nature and development of the moral sentiments, the principles of morality, the natural motives that prompt their actions, or their own true interests either as individuals or as members of society. Is not a mistaken sense of interest the most common cause of actions contrary to the general welfare? Is not the violence of our passions often the result either of habits that we have adopted through miscalculation, or of our ignorance how to restrain them, tame them, deflect them, rule them?

Is not the habit of reflection upon conduct, of listening to the deliverances of reason and conscience upon it, of exercising those gentle feelings which identify our happiness with that of others, the necessary consequence of a well-planned study of morality and of a greater equality in the conditions of the social pact? Will not the free man's sense of his own dignity and a system of education built upon a deeper knowledge of our moral constitution render common to almost every man those principles of strict and unsullied justice, those habits of an active and enlightened benevolence, of a fine and generous sensibility which nature has implanted in the hearts of all and whose flowering waits only upon the favorable influences of enlightenment and freedom? Just as the mathematical and physical sciences tend to improve the arts that we use to satisfy our simplest needs, is it not also part of the necessary order of nature that the moral and political sciences should exercise a similar influence upon the motives that direct our feelings and our actions?

What are we to expect from the perfection of laws and public institutions, consequent upon the progress of those sciences, but the reconciliation, the identification of the interests of each with the interests of all? Has the social art any other aim save that of destroying their apparent opposition? Will not a country's constitution and laws accord best with the rights of reason and nature when the path of virtue is no longer arduous and when the temptations that lead men from it are few and feeble?

Is there any vicious habit, any practice contrary to good faith, any crime, whose origin and first cause cannot be traced back to the legislation, the institutions, the prejudices of the country wherein this habit, this practice, this crime can be observed? In short will not the general welfare that results from the progress of the useful arts once they are grounded on solid theory, or from the progress of legislation once it is rooted in the truths of political science, incline mankind to humanity, benevolence, and justice? In other words, do not all these observations which I propose to develop further in my book, show that the moral goodness of man, the necessary consequence of his constitution, is capable of indefinite perfection like all his other faculties, and that nature has linked together in an unbreakable chain truth, happiness, and virtue?

Among the causes of the progress of the human mind that are of the utmost importance to the general happiness, we must number the complete annihilation of the prejudices that have brought about an inequality of rights between the sexes, an inequality fatal even to the party in which favor it works. It is vain for us to look for a justification of this principle in any differences of physical organization, intellect, or moral sensibility between men and women. This inequality has its origin solely in an abuse of strength, and all the later sophistical attempts that have been made to excuse it are vain.

We shall show how the abolition of customs authorized, laws dictated by this prejudice, would add to the happiness of family life, would encourage the practice of the domestic virtues on which all other virtues are based, how it would favor the progress of education, and how, above all, it would bring about its wider diffusion; for not only would education be extended to women as well as to men, but it can only really be taken proper advantage of when it has the support and encouragement of the mothers of the family. Would not this belated tribute to equity and good sense put an end to a principle only too fecund of injustice, cruelty, and crime, by removing the dangerous conflict between the strongest and most irrepressible of all natural inclinations and man's duty or the interests of society? Would it not produce what has until now been no more than a dream, national manners of a mildness and purity, formed not by proud asceticism, not by hypocrisy, not by the fear of shame or religious terrors but by freely contracted habits that are inspired by nature and acknowledged by reason?

Once people are enlightened they will know that they have the right to dispose of their own life and wealth as they choose; they will gradually learn to regard war as the most dreadful of scourges, the most terrible of crimes. The first wars to disappear will be those into which usurpers have forced their subjects in defense of their pretended hereditary rights.

Nations will learn that they cannot conquer other nations without losing their own liberty; that permanent confederations are their only means of preserving their independence; and that they should seek not power but security. Gradually mercantile prejudices will fade away, and a false sense of commercial interest will lose the fearful power it once had of drenching the earth in blood and of ruining nations under pretext of enriching them. When at last the nations come to agree on the principles of politics and morality, when in their own better interests they invite foreigners to share equally in all the benefits men enjoy either through the bounty of nature or by their own industry, then all the causes that produce and perpetuate national animosities and poison national relations will disappear one by one; and nothing will remain to encourage or even to arouse the fury of war.

Organizations more intelligently conceived than those projects of eternal peace which have filled the leisure and consoled the hearts of certain philosophers will hasten the progress of the brotherhood of nations, and wars between countries will rank with assassinations as freakish atrocities, humiliating and vile in the eyes of nature and staining with indelible opprobrium the country or the age whose annals record them.

When we spoke of the fine arts in Greece, Italy, and France, we observed that it was necessary to distinguish in artistic productions between what belonged properly to the progress of the art itself and what was due only to the talent of the individual artist. We shall here indicate what progress may still be expected in the arts as a result of the progress in philosophy and the sciences, of the increasing number of observations made about the aim, effects, and methods of the arts, of the destruction of those prejudices which have formerly narrowed their sphere and even now hold them within the shackles of authority, shackles that science and philosophy have broken. We shall ask, whether, as some have thought, these means are exhausted, and the arts condemned to an eternal, monotonous imitation of their first models since the most sublime and moving beauty has already been apprehended, the happiest subjects treated, the simplest and most arresting ideas used, the most marked or most generous characters delineated, the liveliest intrinsic passions and their truest or most natural manifestations, the most striking truths and the most brilliant images already exploited.

We shall see that this opinion is a mere prejudice, born of the habit, which is prevalent among artists and men of letters, of judging men, instead of enjoying their words. If the more reflective pleasure of comparing the products of different ages and countries and admiring the success and energy of the efforts of genius will probably be lost, the pleasure to be derived from the actual contemplation of works of art as such will be just as vivid as ever, even though the author may no longer deserve the same credit for having achieved such perfection. As works of art genuinely worthy of preservation increase in number, and become more perfect, each successive generation will devote its attention and admiration to those which really deserve preference, and the rest will unobstrusively fall into oblivion; the pleasure to be derived from the simpler, more striking, more accessible aspects of beauty will exist no less for posterity although they will be found only in the latest works.

The progress of the sciences ensures the progress of the art of education which in turn advances that of the sciences. This reciprocal influence, whose activity is ceaselessly renewed, deserves to be seen as one of the most powerful and active causes working for the perfection of mankind. At the present time a young man on leaving school may know more of the principles of mathematics than Newton ever learned in years of study or discovered by dint of genius, and he may use the calculus with a facility then unknown. The same observation, with certain reservations, applies to all the sciences. As each advances, the methods of expressing a large number of proofs in a more economical fashion and so of making their comprehension an easier matter, advance with it. So, in spite of the progress of science, not only do men of the same ability find themselves at the same age on a level with the existing state of science, but with every generation, that which can be acquired in a certain time with a certain degree of intelligence and a certain amount of concentration will be permanently on the increase, and, as the elementary part of each science to which all men may attain grows and grows, it will more and more include all the knowledge necessary for each man to know for the conduct of the ordinary events of his life, and will support him in the free and independent exercise of his reason.

In the political sciences there are some truths that, with free people (that is to say, with certain generations in all countries) can be of use only if they are widely known and acknowledged. So the influence of these sciences upon the freedom and prosperity of nations must in some degree be measured by the number of truths that, as a result of elementary instruction, are common knowledge; the swelling progress of elementary instruction, connected with the necessary progress of these sciences promises us an improvement in the destiny of the human race, which may be regarded as indefinite, since it can have no other limits than that of this same progress.

We have still to consider two other general methods which will influence both the perfection of education and that of the sciences. One is the more extensive and less imperfect use of what we might call technical methods; the other is the setting up of a universal language.

I mean by technical methods the art of arranging a large number of subjects in a system so that we may immediately grasp their relations, quickly perceive their combinations, and readily form new combinations out of them.

We shall develop the principles and examine the utility of this art, which is still in its infancy, and which, as it improves, will enable us, within the compass of a small chart, to set out what could possibly not be expressed so well in a whole book, or, what is still more valuable, to present isolated facts in such a way as to allow us to deduce their general consequences. We shall see how by means of a small number of these charts, whose use can easily be learned, men who have not been sufficiently educated to be able to absorb details useful to them in ordinary life, may now be able to master them when the need arises, and how these methods may likewise be of benefit to elementary education itself in all those branches where it is concerned either with a regular system of truths or with a series of observations and facts.

A universal language is that which expresses by signs either real objects themselves, or well-defined collections composed of simple and general ideas, which are found to be the same or may arise in a similar form in the minds of all men, or the general relations holding between these ideas, the operations of the human mind, or the operations peculiar to the individual sciences, or the procedures of the arts. So people who become acquainted with these signs, the ways to combine them and the rules for forming them will understand what is written in this language and will be able to read it as easily as their own language.

It is obvious that this language might be used to set out the theory of a science or the rules of an art, to describe a new observation or experiment, the invention of a procedure, the discovery of a truth or a method; and that, as in algebra, when one has to make use of a new sign, those already known provide the means of explaining its import.

Such a language has not the disadvantages of a scientific idiom different from the vernacular. We have already observed that the use of such an idiom would necessarily divide society into two unequal classes, the one composed of men who, understanding this language, would possess the key to all the sciences, the other of men who, unable to acquire it, would therefore find themselves almost completely unable to acquire enlightenment. In contrast to this, a universal language would be learned, like that of algebra, along with the science itself; the sign would be learned at the same time as the object, idea, or operation that it designates. He who, having mastered the elements of a science, would like to know more of it, would find in books not only truths he could understand by means of the signs whose import he has learned, but also the explanation of such further signs as he needs in order to go on to other truths.

We shall show that the formation of such a language, if confined to the expression of those simple, precise propositions which form the system of a science or the practice of an art, is no chimerical scheme; that even at the present time it could be readily introduced to deal with a large number of objects; and that, indeed, the chief obstacle that would prevent its extension to others would be the humiliation of having to admit how very few precise ideas and accurate, unambiguous notions we actually possess.

We shall show that this language, ever improving and broadening its scope all the while, would be the means of giving to every subject embraced by the human intelligence a precision and a rigor that would make knowledge of the truth easy and error almost impossible. Then the progress of every science would be as sure as that of mathematics, and the propositions that compose it would acquire a geometrical certainty, as far, that is, as is possible granted the nature of its aim and method.

All the causes that contribute to the perfection of the human race, all the means that ensure it must by their very nature exercise a perpetual influence and always increase their sphere of action—the proofs of this we have given and in the great work they will derive additional force from elaboration. We may conclude then that the perfectibility of man is indefinite. Meanwhile we have considered him as possessing the natural faculties and organization that he has at present. How much greater would be the certainty, how much vaster the scheme of our hopes if we could believe that these natural faculties themselves and this organization could also be improved? This is the last question that remains for us to ask ourselves.

Organic perfectibility or deterioration among the various strains in the vegetable and animal kingdoms can be regarded as one of the general laws of nature. This law also applies to the human race. No one can doubt that, as preventive medicine improves and food and housing become healthier, as a way of life is established that develops our physical powers by exercise without ruining them by excess, as the two most virulent causes of deterioration, misery and excessive wealth, are eliminated, the average length of human life will be increased and a better health and a stronger physical constitution will be ensured. The improvement of medical practice, which will become more efficacious with the progress of reason and of the social order, will mean the end of infectious and hereditary diseases and illnesses brought on by climate, food, or working conditions. It is reasonable to hope that all other diseases may likewise disappear as their distant causes are discovered. Would it be absurd then to suppose that this perfection of the human species might be capable of indefinite progress; that the day will come when death will be due only to extraordinary accidents or to the decay of the vital forces, and that ultimately the average span between birth and decay will have no assignable value? Certainly man will not become immortal, but will not the interval between the first breath that he draws and the time when in the natural course of events, without disease or accident, he expires, increase indefinitely? Since we are now speaking of a progress that can be represented with some accuracy in figures or on a graph, we shall take this opportunity of explaining the two meanings that can be attached to the word *indefinite*.

In truth, this average span of life which we suppose will increase indefinitely as time passes, may grow in conformity either with a law such that it continually approaches a limitless length but without ever reaching it, or with a law such that through the centuries it reaches a length greater than any determinate quantity that we may assign to it as its limit. In the latter case such an increase is truly indefinite in the strictest sense of the word, since there is no term on this side of which it must of necessity stop. In the former case it is equally indefinite in relation to us, if we cannot fix the limit it always approaches without ever reaching, and particularly if, knowing only that it will never stop, we are ignorant in which of the two senses the term *indefinite* can be applied to it. Such is the present condition of our knowledge as far as the perfectibility of the human race is concerned; such is the sense in which we may call it indefinite.

In the example under consideration, we are bound to believe that the average length of human life will forever increase unless this is prevented by physical revolutions; we do not know what the limit is which it can never exceed. We cannot tell even whether the general laws of nature have determined such a limit or not.

But are not our physical faculties and the strength, dexterity, and acuteness of our senses to be numbered among the qualities whose perfection in the individual may be transmitted? Observation of the various breeds of domestic animals inclines us to believe that they are, and we can confirm this by direct observation of the human race.

Finally may we not extend such hopes to the intellectual and moral faculties? May not our parents, who transmit to us the benefits or disadvantages of their constitution, and from whom we receive our shape and features, as well as our tendencies to certain physical affections, hand on to us also that part of the physical organization which determines the intellect, the power of the brain, the ardor of the soul, or the moral sensibility? Is it not probable that education, in perfecting these qualities, will at the same time influence, modify, and perfect the organization itself? Analogy, investigation of the human faculties, and the study of certain facts all seem to give substance to such conjectures which would further push back the boundaries of our hopes.

These are the questions with which we shall conclude this final stage. How consoling for the philosopher who laments the errors, the crimes, the injustices which still pollute the earth and of which he is often the victim is this view of the human race, emancipated from its shackles, released from the empire of fate and from that of the enemies of its progress, advancing with a firm and sure step along the path of truth, virtue, and happiness! It is the contemplation of this prospect that rewards him for all his efforts to assist the progress of reason and the defense of liberty. He dares to regard these strivings as part of the eternal chain of human destiny; and in this persuasion he is filled with the true delight of virtue and the pleasure of having done some lasting good which fate can never destroy by a sinister stroke of revenge, by calling back the reign of slavery and prejudice. Such contemplation is for him an asylum, in which the memory of his persecutors cannot pursue him; there he lives in thought with man restored to his natural rights and dignity, forgets man tormented and corrupted by greed, fear or envy; there he lives with his peers in an Elysium created by reason and graced by the purest pleasures known to the love of mankind.